Decolonising the Histo

"This is an important book at a time when colleagues across education are scrutinising their work, seeking to increase diversity and to build a balanced equitable learning experience for all. Moncrieffe argues for the importance of building critical consciousness with regard to ethnicity. His original research with Primary PGCE students reveals the Eurocentricity of many trainee teachers. He illustrates the way in which this viewpoint without disruption through consideration of alternative stories, will continue to inform future teaching in their classrooms. Moncrieffe shows how important it is to view history through a cross-cultural lens. He reflects on events in recent history in this country and shows how they may be considered differently. I recommend this book to all those training to teach and to those keen to revisit their predisposed assumptions about what should be taught in the primary history curriculum."
—Dame Alison Peacock, Chief Executive, *The Chartered College of Teaching, UK*

"This book is a timely, and above all, practical guide to the transformation of Britain's primary school history curriculum. It will be an invaluable tool for teachers and trainers as well as a map for future debates over the importance of history in the making of national identity."
—Professor Paul Gilroy, *Institute of Advanced Studies, University College London, UK*

"Decolonising the history curriculum is essential reading for primary school teachers. Dr Moncrieffe's succinct interrogation of the socio-political climate that has informed the actual, implied and applied key stage two history curriculum utilises a decolonising framework to expose the impacts of institutionalised whiteness in the teaching profession as well as the possibilities for transformation. Decolonising the history curriculum speaks directly to the need for a reclaiming of the purpose of education from neoliberal and neoconservative agendas to trauma-sensitive social justice agendas that enable children to recognise and reckon with our collective past in order to construct a better future."
—Camile Kumar, Race Equality Policy Specialist, *National Education Union, UK*

Marlon Lee Moncrieffe

Decolonising the History Curriculum

Euro-centrism and Primary Schooling

Marlon Lee Moncrieffe
School of Education
University of Brighton
Brighton, UK

ISBN 978-3-030-57947-0   ISBN 978-3-030-57945-6 (eBook)
https://doi.org/10.1007/978-3-030-57945-6

© The Editor(s) (if applicable) and The Author(s), under exclusive licence to Springer Nature Switzerland AG 2020
This work is subject to copyright. All rights are solely and exclusively licensed by the Publisher, whether the whole or part of the material is concerned, specifically the rights of translation, reprinting, reuse of illustrations, recitation, broadcasting, reproduction on microfilms or in any other physical way, and transmission or information storage and retrieval, electronic adaptation, computer software, or by similar or dissimilar methodology now known or hereafter developed.
The use of general descriptive names, registered names, trademarks, service marks, etc. in this publication does not imply, even in the absence of a specific statement, that such names are exempt from the relevant protective laws and regulations and therefore free for general use.
The publisher, the authors and the editors are safe to assume that the advice and information in this book are believed to be true and accurate at the date of publication. Neither the publisher nor the authors or the editors give a warranty, expressed or implied, with respect to the material contained herein or for any errors or omissions that may have been made. The publisher remains neutral with regard to jurisdictional claims in published maps and institutional affiliations.

Cover credit: Cover pattern © Melisa Hasan

This Palgrave Pivot imprint is published by the registered company Springer Nature Switzerland AG.
The registered company address is: Gewerbestrasse 11, 6330 Cham, Switzerland

"Three kisses for Rossi."

Foreword

In this book, Marlon, presents a passionate argument to teach a history that better reflects the diversity of past experiences. In particular, he deals with a significant issue in history education, namely what historical content makes it into the curriculum and gets taught to children in this country. This matters for numerous reasons. Firstly, what gets included in the curriculum, and perhaps more importantly, what gets excluded from the curriculum, sends out powerful messages to young people about what is valued. Excluding the presence and voice of people from minority ethnic backgrounds therefore sends out a clear signal to all students that somehow the past activities of these groups is not worthy of attention. Secondly, the knock-on effect of this can serve to alienate and disengage young people from minority ethnic backgrounds from education generally. Why should young people engage with a curriculum from which they are ignored and absent, or if present are often cast as victims of slavery and oppression. Thirdly a curriculum that is predominantly White (and largely male as well) cannot be representative of the past. Modern society is diverse, yet past societies were also inherently diverse. The first recorded presence of Black people in the British Isles dates to Roman times, several centuries before Anglo-Saxons came to these shores, yet this is not often appreciated. Recent historical scholarship is shedding new light on the presence of minority ethnic groups in the UK throughout the centuries, showing a long history of settlement and movement. To ignore the fact that the past is diverse is therefore to present young people with a distorted view of this past.

One of the main arguments in this book is to highlight the way that history education policy documents serve to sideline the presence of minority ethnic groups, and instead portray a White Anglo-centric view of the past. These documents reflect a dominate discourse around 'Our Island Story'. The use of the notion of historical consciousness helps to understand how this happens, but also how the way we view the past could be different. It can be argued that historical consciousness reflects the way that individuals make sense of the past to explain their present, and ultimately shapes what they see as possible futures. Certain forms of historical consciousness serve to reinforce a narrow understanding of the past, whereas other forms open a wider world of understanding. Working with primary trainee teachers, and using examples of recent 'cross-cultural encounters', Marlon is looking to challenge their preconceptions about the past and provide different ways of seeing the past. This matters because much of the attention about rethinking the history curriculum has focused on secondary schools, whereas the work here is with primary trainee teachers. They are often not history specialists, so may be unaware of the debates discussed in this book. Also, most primary school teachers in the UK are White, and as is explained 'White privilege' often means people do not appreciate how 'Whiteness' dominates their thinking. Getting White trainee teachers to question their assumptions about the diverse nature of the past is therefore a crucial activity in enabling them to consider how to teach a more representative past. This in turn should allow children to develop a more nuanced, sophisticated, and complex understanding of the past. Given the current emphasis on 'British values' in schools, surely a curriculum that looks at the range of past experiences and the struggles of different individuals and groups, can only support a developing understanding of issues such individual liberty and respect for all.

This book therefore addresses several genuinely important questions in the current education system. History offers us a chance to explore the fascinating array of human activity, which helps us understand ourselves better, but we can only do that if we create a curriculum that allows us to explore a past that better reflects the diverse range of experiences.

Institute of Education, University of Reading,
Reading, UK   Rebecca Harris

Acknowledgements

Mother, your voice in strong in this.

For Audrey and Rose-Marie:
"The purpose is in the dream.
And to dream is the only way."

Thank you to Rebecca Harris for your support and expertise. Thank you to Tara Dean and Andrew Church for the time given to complete this book. Thank you to Eleanor Christie and Rebecca Wyde at Palgrave Macmillan.

Contents

1 Introduction — 1

2 'Epistemic Violence' in the History Curriculum — 13

3 White Trainee-Teachers Reproduce Eurocentric and White-British Histories — 25

4 Orienting with Historical Consciousness — 47

5 Centring the Black Experience in Key Stage 2 Primary School British History — 57

6 Transforming White-British Trainee-Teachers' Thinking Through Black-British History — 77

7 Opportunity, Action and Commitment — 85

Index — 91

List of Tables

Table 3.1	Identities of trainee-teachers	31
Table 4.1	Typologies of historical consciousness	48
Table 6.1	Identities of trainee-teachers focus-group discussion	79

CHAPTER 1

Introduction

Abstract This chapter states that the aims and contents of the Key Stage 2 primary school history curriculum for teaching and learning pupils aged 7–11 years old are exclusively Eurocentric for the cultural reproduction of White supremacy (Whiteness) in schools, classrooms, and society in general. Decolonising the curriculum is introduced as a concept that seeks to dismantle the dominance of 'Whiteness' in all phases of education. Typologies for decolonising the curriculum are presented as: the 'revolutionary approach'; the 'radical approach'; and, the 'gestural-superficial approach'. It is argued that decolonising the history curriculum is necessary for helping with repressing the increasing divisiveness of ethnic nationalism's political and social influence on society. This has been seen recently through 'Brexit'; the institutional ignorance understood by the 'Windrush Scandal'; and the egregious disparities of patient treatment according to racial group evidenced by Covid-19 research. Finally, a critical framework for decolonising the Key Stage 2 primary school history curriculum is shared as the focal point of this book.

Keywords Decolonising • Eurocentrism • Whiteness • White narcissism • Ethnic nationalism

© The Author(s) 2020
M. L. Moncrieffe, *Decolonising the History Curriculum*,
https://doi.org/10.1007/978-3-030-57945-6_1

Curriculum, Eurocentrism and Whiteness

The Key Stage 2 primary school history curriculum (DfE 2013) for teaching and learning is framed by Eurocentric aims and contents dominated by 'Whiteness' (Eddo-Lodge 2017; Di Angelo 2011; Frankenburg 1993). I am speaking about 'Whiteness' as a narcissistic existential orientation from which White people (some consciously, some unconsciously) view the world as a norm by which 'the other' (Said 1978) non-White person is judged. 'White narcissism' (Matias 2016) means White people seeing themselves only, as universal human beings who can represent all of human experience (Eddo-Lodge 2017; Delgado and Stefanic 2012; Di Angelo 2011; Gillborn 2008; Fanon 1963, 1967/2008; Bhabha 2004; Ladson-Billings 1998; McIntyre 1997; Frankenburg 1993; Said 1978).

Attention in this book is given to what I see as 'Whiteness' in the Key Stage 2 primary school history curriculum aims and contents. I see these aims and contents as 'hegemonic', where they direct primary school teachers to teach history for the purposes of cultural reproduction to their pupils through exclusive White-British stories of the past as relevant to knowing about present times, and the future. The 'Whiteness' that I see leads my concerns about structural racism functioning through the collective mindset of White-British teachers in primary school education. The dominant White-British teacher workforce in primary schools (DfE 2020) implementing their lesson planning and teaching uncritically and aligned to the same Eurocentric biases as the Key Stage 2 primary school history curriculum means that they reify and perpetuate ideological associations with knowledge, education, and progress through 'Whiteness' (Chantiluke 2018). This complicity with 'Whiteness' becomes so widespread (Eddo-Lodge 2017) that White-British teachers fail to even notice. The dominance of 'Whiteness' allows White pupils to see their backgrounds and perspectives as objective and representative of norms articulated by the curriculum, as opposed to non-White pupils who are disconnected by this exposure to British history (Charles 2019; Chantiluke 2018; Hawkey and Prior 2011; Smart 2010; Grever et al. 2008; Maylor et al. 2007; Traille 2007). This means that White pupils are positioned at an advantage in their learning about British history, in comparison to non-White pupils. This inequality of access to equitable knowledge through the formal national history curriculum is a major concern of this book.

Decolonising Curriculum Knowledge (Whiteness)

Modern society is based upon the hierarchies of Eurocentrism in which the creation of anti-Blackness is essential (Andrews 2018a, b). Decolonising the curriculum knowledge means to decentre the 'Whiteness' of Eurocentrism for dismantling racism and oppression (Milne 2019). Intervention and action to decolonise 'Whiteness' in curriculum, education, teaching and learning is not a new one (Bhambra et al. 2018). Anti-racist activism work through minority-ethnic groups and Black parents in Britain since the 1960s has included supplementary Saturday schools with Black-led, Black-centred and community-based education to counter intrinsic racial biases of the White-British education system (Chetty 2020; Race 2020; Chantiluke 2018; Andrews 2013). These schools emerged because of the failure by successive governments to encourage curriculum policies to combat cultural ignorance, ethnocentric attitudes and racism in society (Chantiluke 2018; Andrews 2013; Tomlinson 2005).

The campaign for decolonising the curriculum is a struggle that continues today across all phases of education. It has been amplified in the UK, particularly through the "Why is my Curriculum White Campaign?" in 2014 by students of University of College London, and the 'Rhodes must fall' campaign by students of University of Oxford (Charles 2019; Chantiluke et al. 2018; Sabaratnam 2017). Student grievances were directed at what Peters (2015, p. 641) describes as 'the lack of awareness that the curriculum is comprised of 'White ideas' by 'White authors', and is a result of colonialism that has normalised Whiteness and made Blackness invisible'. Steinburg (2020) provides caution to this decolonial movement by suggesting that any acknowledgment given to the construct of a Eurocentric curriculum as the starting point for thinking about reinventing knowledge is in itself a colonial act. However, decolonising the curriculum means to cause 'epistemic discomfort' by decentring Whiteness through critical curriculum thinking (Harris 2020). This is a route to 'epistemic innovation' in teaching, learning and education for supporting praxis to move beyond the 'colonial zero-point' (Domínguez 2019).

Typologies for Decolonising the Curriculum

I see both possibilities and problems with decolonising the curriculum through my own conception of three types of thinking and action: the 'revolutionary' approach; the 'radical' approach; and, the 'gestural-superficial' approach.

A starting point for seeing and understanding the 'revolutionary' approach is Andrews' (2018a, b) paradigm of 'Black radicalism'. It is one in which he states a vision of 'Blackness' that would include 'all of our cultural, social and representational forms rooted in providing for those suffering the worst oppression' (Andrews 2018a, b, p. 297). He argues: 'Freedom can only be found in overturning the Western imperial status quo' (Andrews 2018a, b, p. 284). This perspective meets with Mazama's (2003) presentation of Afrocentrism, a paradigm for seeing and knowing about the world and its history in opposition to Eurocentrism. This is a paradigm of thought which professes a canon of knowledge for the sake of liberation (Charles 2019; Mazama 2003). Afrocentrism has been criticised for its essentialist discourses that echo the colonising Eurocentric ideologies that it seeks to dismantle (Joyce 2003).

A 'radical' approach to decolonising the curriculum through teaching and learning can be seen through 'transformative critical multicultural education' (May and Sleeter 2010; Banks 1997, 2009; McLaren 2002). This seeks to shift what counts as knowledge away from the dominant ethnic groups' vantage point, in order to embody the lives and histories of marginalised ethnic groups in society (Sleeter 2010). It is an embedded and sustained approach in teaching and learning that transforms the basic assumptions of Eurocentrism in the curriculum (Moncrieffe 2019). However, 'transformative critical multicultural education' is open to criticism, for working within the Eurocentric framework of curriculum that it seeks to change.

My seeing the 'gestural-superficial' approach to decolonising the curriculum comes through notions of 'diversification' of the curriculum (Bird and Pitman 2020). This has been through amendments to university course study reading lists for the inclusion of Black and Asian writers. A further example of this 'gestural-superficial' approach has been through what I have seen in the rare appearance of Black or Asian Professors of Education, unearthed by institutional management to provide key-note lectures on the themes of 'Whiteness' and curriculum 'diversification' for an audience of majority White colleagues. I also see the hypothetical format of 'unconscious bias training' as another example of the 'gestural-superficial' approach to decolonising the curriculum for teaching and learning about race-equality. I acknowledge that what I deem to be 'gestural-superficial' may be argued as 'radical' approaches to decolonising the curriculum, with aims to challenge and to change narrow

White-cultural perspectives embedded in dominant White institutions of education. However, where these approaches are progressed as 'one-off' tick-box actions, or temporal procedures that become lost after fulfilling the aims of institutional neo-liberal projects, this is where the 'gestural-superficial' categorisation is the right one. Still, for proponents of decolonising the curriculum, there are even greater societal challenges to tackle alongside what may be falsities in the 'gestural-superficial' White-led institutional approach.

Ethnic Nationalism

The ideology behind the United Kingdom's decision to depart from the European Union (Brexit) in 2020 was won by the influence of traditionalist White-British ethnic-nationalist orientations with culture and society (Lammy 2020). This ethnic nationalism orientation is interested solely in the preservation and celebration of White-British culture and histories as representations of Britishness in past, present and future (Moncrieffe and Moncrieffe 2019). This type of ethnic nationalism is the epitome of 'White narcissism', with origins both traced and linked to White-British supremacists of the past and present including: Oswald Mosely, Enoch Powell, Nigel Farage and Nick Griffin. Where this ethnic-nationalism perspective can strongly influence British government policies, all non-White British citizens associated with 'multiculturalism' become targeted and labelled as problems and outsiders in their own country of residence and birth. The recent 'Windrush Scandal' (Bulman 2020; Agerholm 2018; Gentleman 2018) provides a clear example of this treatment. Many African-Caribbean people (Black-British immigrants) of the West Indies who had migrated to Britain in the mid-twentieth century following an invitation by the British Labour government, having lived and worked in Britain as citizens for most of their lives, have since 2013 faced the ignominy of Conservative government enforced deportation.

This pervasive influence of ethnic nationalist discourses that are apparent in British society must be challenged through education, and decolonising the curriculum in schools. Advanced forms of teacher-training and professional development are required for pupils to learn about the stories of ethnogenesis and diversity of British people found in British history. Perceptions about the statutory teaching and learning in schools of fundamental British values (DfE 2014) such as 'tolerance' and 'mutual respect' must be transformed and considered more significantly through the ethnogenesis and diversity of people migrating and settling on the British Isles over the ages. We can advance notions of fundamental British values by exploring the stories of our cross-cultural encounters with each other over the ages.

'POST' COVID-19 CHALLENGES

The devastating effects of the Covid-19 world pandemic since 2020 has exposed the vulnerability of our human existence. The Covid-19 pandemic has also starkly revealed the inequality of British society's ethnic multicultural co-existence, specifically where it was reported that Covid-19 patients of Black and Asian backgrounds have been treated less favourably than White people; and are four times more likely to die from the virus than White people (Croxford 2020; Downey 2020; Godin 2020; Liverpool 2020). The Covid-19 crisis has exposed the privilege of 'Whiteness' in British society. This shows that anti-racist knowledge and education for society must be advanced.

CRITICAL FRAMEWORK

Decolonising curriculum knowledge (Whiteness) of the Key Stage 2 primary school history curriculum must involve a creative dissemination of alternative ways in seeing the past as relevant to knowing about present times, and the future. Education, knowledge and understanding must be given to young people about the cross-cultural encounters that people of British Isles have endured with each other concerning their ethnic and cultural differences, and how as a result of these, British society has been forced to speak and learn about the need for 'tolerance' and 'mutual respect' in our culturally diverse co-existence. Cultivating knowledge about cross-cultural encounters between the peoples of multiethnic and multicultural Britain must begin with teaching and learning history in the primary school classroom. To support and to advance this, the school curriculum for teaching and learning about British history must be decolonised, transformed, and made to become inclusive for all pupils.

This book provides a fourfold critical framework for decolonising the Key Stage 2 primary school history curriculum. Firstly, an undoing of the presumptively White-British island story; next, revealing the insular experiences, knowledge and training of pre-dominantly White-British primary school teachers; from this, an introduction and development of Black-British oral histories that capture and personalise events that mark alternative significant histories of minority-ethnic groups; and finally, demonstrating the socialisation of White-British primary school teachers into a critical race-based way of thinking about history. Chapter 2 gives a sense of attitude towards race-equality held by past and present British governments, and on how they are orientated with teaching and learning about British history through curriculum design. The chapter develops an understanding on why a Neo-Conservative White-British master narrative has been reasserted today as a dominant educational discourse of the history curriculum. The impact of this curriculum design is argued as 'epistemic violence' (Spivak 1999). This can be observed where the 'Purpose of Study', aims and contents of the history curriculum (DfE 2013) imposes a Eurocentric discourse, suffocating any explicit opportunity for teaching and learning the story of Britain's past through multicultural British histories. Following this, Chap. 3 states the biggest challenge to decolonising the curriculum is in attempting to reframe a Eurocentric mindset held by the majority of White-British teachers; the default position from which they begin to think about teaching the story of Britain's past. An argument to support this claim is made through an examination of how Eurocentric and White-British only histories of the Key Stage 2 primary school history curriculum are most likely to be reproduced in schools as cultural hegemony by White-British primary school history trainee-teachers. Chapter 4 extends its examination of White-British-trainee primary school history teachers' thinking, by presenting their perspectives of British history according to their orientations with 'historical consciousness' (Rüsen 2004). This is to illustrate how White-British primary school history trainee-teachers are positioned in their view of what is most important to them for teaching and learning the story of British history in the Key Stage 2 classroom. This also provides an understanding on the extent to which their thinking serves to either reify or decolonise the discourses of Eurocentrism found in the Key Stage 2 primary school history curriculum. In Chap. 5 the Black-British experience is centred as a starting point for decolonising Eurocentrism and 'Whiteness' in the Key Stage 2 primary school history curriculum. In this chapter, I share my memories and those of my mother's. I present our interpretations of cross-cultural encounters involving our migrant African-Caribbean minority-ethnic group people, and White-Britain in 1981 in Brixton, London. These recent experiences of cross-cultural encounters are juxtaposed with Eurocentric similarities from the distant past that are stated for statutory teaching and learning by the Key Stage 2 primary school history curriculum aims and contents i.e. Anglo-Saxon and Viking 'struggles' as cross-cultural encounters. Following this, Chap. 6 sees White-British primary school history trainee-teachers providing their critical thoughts on using Black-British history as the central stimulus for teaching and pupils learning. This is in connection with the 'Purpose of Study', aims and contents of the Key Stage 2 primary school history curriculum. Finally, Chap. 7 gives examples of evidenced based research and knowledge for decolonising the curriculum provided through teaching and learning about mass-migration and settlement to Britain over the ages. Critical curriculum thinking (Harris 2020) is advocated as an opportunity for action in advancing practice and pedagogy for decolonising Eurocentrism in the Key Stage 2 history curriculum (DfE 2013).

The Black-British Voice

It is acknowledged that the Black-British voice presented in this book cannot present the 'total reality' of all non-White British people in their life experiences and encounters with 'Whiteness' and Eurocentrism. Still, I see that this Black-British voice and experience is portable to situations where some of the identity dynamics are different, but the effects of White-supremacist Eurocentrism look familiar. For example, the vilification and 'othering' (Said 1978) of all British Muslims as a raced, racialised and 'radicalised' category of people by the media discourses of 'Whiteness' following the 7/7 London terrorist attacks (Race 2015, 2019). The social, cultural and educational experiences of British Muslims and other non-White British citizens in their cross-cultural encounters with 'Whiteness' can be seen in congruency to examples of White-British and Black-British cross-cultural dichotomy presented in this book.

References

Agerholm, H. (2018). *Windrush: Government Admits 83 British Citizens May Have Been Wrongfully Deported Due to Scandal But Will Only Apologise to 18.* Retrieved November 29, 2019, from https://www.independent.co.uk/news/uk/home-news/windrush-government-deportations-british-citizens-uk-caribbean-home-office-rudd-javid-a8501076.html

Andrews, K. (2013). *Resisting Racism: Race, Inequality, and the Black Supplementary School Movement.* London: Institute of Education Press.

Andrews, K. (2018a). *Back to Black: Retelling Black Radicalism for the 21st Century*. London: Zed Books.
Andrews, K. (2018b). Foreword. In R. Chantiluke, B. Kwomba, & N. Athinangamso (Eds.), *Rhodes Must Fall: The Struggle to Decolonise The Racist Heart of Empire*. London: Zed Books.
Banks, J. A. (1997). *Educating Citizens in a Multicultural Society* (Multicultural Education Series). New York: Teachers College Press.
Banks, J. A. (Ed.). (2009). *The Routledge International Companion to Multicultural Education*. Abingdon: Routledge.
Bhabha, H. (2004). *The Location of Culture*. London: Routledge.
Bhambra, G. K., Gebrial, D., & Nişancıoğlu, K. (2018). *Decolonising the University*. London: Pluto Press.
Bird, K. S., & Pitman, L. (2020). How Diverse is Your Reading List? Exploring Issues of Representation and Decolonisation in the UK. *Higher Education, 79*(5), 903–920. https://doi.org/10.1007/s10734-019-00446-9.
Bulman, M. (2020). *Home Office Showed 'Institutional Ignorance and Thoughtlessness' Towards Race, Windrush Report Finds*. Retrieved March 23, 2020, from https://www.independent.co.uk/news/uk/home-news/windrush-report-scandal-generation-news-racism-latest-a9411186.html
Chantiluke, R. (2018). British Values' and Decolonial Resistance in the Classroom. In R. Chantiluke, B. Kwomba, & N. Athinangamso (Eds.), *Rhodes Must Fall: The Struggle to Decolonise The Racist Heart of Empire*. London: Zed Books.
Chantiluke, R., Kwomba, B., & Athinangamso, N. (2018). *Rhodes Must Fall: The Struggle to Decolonise The Racist Heart of Empire*. London: Zed Books.
Charles, M. (2019). Effective Teaching and Learning: Decolonizing the Curriculum. *Journal of Black Studies, 50*(8), 731–766. https://doi.org/10.1177/0021934719885631.
Chetty, D. (2020). A Personal Journey into Decolonising the Curriculum and Addressing 'White Fragility'. In M. L. Moncrieffe, R. Race, & R. Harris (Eds.), *Decolonising the Curriculum – Transnational Perspectives, Research Intelligence Issue 142, Spring 2020* (p. 10). London: British Educational Research Association. https://www.bera.ac.uk/publication/spring-2020.
Croxford, R. (2020). *Coronavirus Cases to be Tracked by Ethnicity*. Retrieved May 7, 2020, from https://www.bbc.co.uk/news/health-52338101
Delgado, R., & Stefanic, J. (2012). *Critical Race Theory: An Introduction, Second Edition*. New York: New York University Press.
Department for Education (DfE). (2013, July). History Programmes of Study: Key Stages 1 and 2. National Curriculum in England. In *The National Curriculum in Britain Framework Document*. London: DfE.
Department for Education (DfE). (2014). *Promoting Fundamental British Values as Part of SMSC in Schools: Departmental Advice for Maintained Schools*. London: Department for Education.

Department for Education (DfE). (2020). *Ethnicity Facts and Figures: School Teacher Workforce*. Retrieved March 4, 2020, from https://www.ethnicity-facts-figures.service.gov.uk/workforce-and-business/workforce-diversity/school-teacher-workforce/latest

Di Angelo, R. (2011). White Fragility. *International Journal of Critical Pedagogy, 3*(3), 54–70. https://libjournal.uncg.edu/ijcp/article/viewFile/249/116.

Domínguez, M. (2019). Decolonial Innovation in Teacher Development: Praxis Beyond the Colonial Zero-Point. *Journal of Education for Teaching, 45*(1), 47–62. https://doi.org/10.1080/02607476.2019.1550605.

Downey, A. (2020). *Public Health England to Review Impact of Ethnicity on Covid-19 Outcomes*. Retrieved May 13, 2020, from https://www.digitalhealth.net/2020/05/public-health-england-to-review-impact-of-ethnicity-on-covid-19-outcomes/

Eddo-Lodge. (2017). *Why I'm No Longer Talking to White People About Race*. London: Bloomsbury Circus.

Fanon, F. (1963). *The Wretched of the Earth*. New York: Penguin Press.

Fanon, F. (2008). *Black Skin, White Masks*. London: Pluto Press. (Original work published in 1967).

Frankenburg, R. (1993). *White Women, Race Matters: The Social Construction of Whiteness*. New York: Taylor Francis.

Gentleman, A. (2018). *'My Life is in Ruins': Wrongly Deported Windrush People Facing Fresh Indignity*. Retrieved November 20, 2019, from https://www.theguardian.com/uk-news/2018/sep/10/windrush-people-wrongly-deported-jamaica-criminal-offence

Gillborn, D. (2008). *Racism and Education: Coincidence or Conspiracy?* London: Routledge.

Godin, M. (2020). *Black and Asian People are 2 to 3 Times More Likely to Die of COVID-19, U.K. Study Finds*. Retrieved May 7, 2020, from https://time.com/5832807/coronavirus-race-analysis-uk/

Grever, M., Haydn, T., & Ribbens, K. (2008). Identity and School History: The Perspective of Young People from the Netherlands and Britain. *British Journal of Educational Studies, 56*(1), 76–94. https://doi.org/10.1111/j.1467-8527.2008.00396.x.

Harris, R. (2020). Decolonising the History Curriculum. In M. L. Moncrieffe, R. Race, & R. Harris (Eds.), *Decolonising the Curriculum – Transnational Perspectives, Research Intelligence Issue 142, Spring 2020* (p. 16). London: British Educational Research Association. https://www.bera.ac.uk/publication/spring-2020.

Hawkey, K., & Prior, J. (2011). History, Memory Cultures and Meaning in the Classroom. *Journal of Curriculum Studies, 43*(2), 231–247. https://doi.org/10.1080/00220272.2010.516022.

Joyce, J. (2003). African-Centred Scholarship: Interrogating Black Studies, Pan-Africanism and Afrocentricity. In C. Davies (Ed.), *Decolonising the Academy: African Diaspora Studies* (pp. 125–147). Trenton, NJ: Africa New World Press.

Ladson-Billings, G. (1998). Just What is Critical Race Theory and What's it Doing in a Nice Field Like Education? *Qualitative Studies in Education, 11*(1), 7–24. https://doi.org/10.1080/095183998236863.

Lammy, D. (2020). *Tribes: How Our Need to Belong Can Make or Break the Good Society*. London: Constable.

Liverpool, L. (2020). *An Unequal Society Means Covid-19 is Hitting Ethnic Minorities Harder*. Retrieved May 5, 2020, from https://www.newscientist.com/article/2241278-an-unequal-society-means-covid-19-is-hitting-ethnic-minorities-harder/#ixzz6LlTA7hx4

Matias, C. E. (2016). *Feeling White. Cultural Pluralism Democracy, Socio-Environmental Justice & Education*. Rotterdam: Sense Publishers.

May, S., & Sleeter, C. E. (2010). *Critical Multiculturalism: Theory and Praxis*. London: Routledge.

Maylor, U., Read, B., Mendick, H., Ross, A., & Rollock, N. (2007). *Diversity and Citizenship in the Curriculum: Research Review*. London: The Institute for Policy Studies in Education London Metropolitan University.

Mazama, A. (2003). *The Afrocentric Paradigm*. Trenton, NJ: Africa World Press.

McIntyre, A. (1997). *Making Meaning of Whiteness: Exploring Racial Identity with White Teachers*. New York: State University of New York Press.

McLaren, P. (2002). White Terror and Oppositional Agency: Towards a Critical Multiculturalism. In *Critical Pedagogy and Predatory Culture* (pp. 131–158). London: Routledge.

Milne, A. (2019). *White Supremacy in Our Classrooms*. Retrieved May 5, 2020, from https://educationcentral.co.nz/opinion-ann-milne-White-supremacy-in-our-classrooms/

Moncrieffe, M. L. (2019). An Approach to Decolonising the National Curriculum for Key Stage 2 History in Initial Teacher Education. In M. L. Moncrieffe, Y. Asare, R. Dunford, & H. Youssef (Eds.), *Decolonising the Curriculum – Teaching and Learning about Race Equality, Issue 1, July 2019* (p. 12). Brighton: Centre for Learning and Teaching, University of Brighton. https://cris.brighton.ac.uk/ws/portalfiles/portal/6443632/Decolonising_the_curriculum_MONCRIEFFE_32_pages_4th_July.pdf.

Moncrieffe, M., & Moncrieffe, A. (2019). An Examination of Imagery Used to Represent Fundamental British Values and British Identity on Primary School Display Boards. *London Review of Education, 17*(1), 52–69. https://doi.org/10.18546/LRE.17.1.05.

Peters, M. A. (2015). Why is My Curriculum White? *Educational Philosophy and Theory, 47,* 641–646. https://doi.org/10.1080/00131857.2015.1037227.

Race, R. (2015). *Multiculturalism and Education* (2nd ed.). London: Bloomsbury.

Race, R. (2019). Promoting and Advancing Multicultural Dialogues in Education. *Journal of Dialogue Studies, 6*, 65–71.

Race, R. (2020). Integration and Decolonising the Curriculum. In M. L. Moncrieffe, R. Race, & R. Harris (Eds.), *Decolonising the Curriculum – Transnational Perspectives, Research Intelligence Issue 142, Spring 2020* (p. 20). London: British Educational Research Association. https://www.bera.ac.uk/publication/spring-2020.

Rüsen, J. (2004). Historical Consciousness: Narrative Structure, Moral Function, and Ontogenetic Development. In P. Seixas (Ed.), *Theorizing Historical Consciousness* (pp. 63–85). Toronto: University of Toronto Press.

Sabaratnam, M. (2017). *Decolonising Intervention: International Statebuilding in Mozambique*. London: Rowman & Littlefield International.

Said, E. (1978). *Orientalism*. London: Penguin Books.

Sleeter, C. (2010). Decolonizing Curriculum. *Curriculum Inquiry, 40*(2), 193–203. https://doi.org/10.1111/j.1467-873X.2010.00477.x?journalCode=rcui20.

Smart, D. (2010). Going to the pictures: Learning to See the Life Stories of Minorities Within Majority Narratives. In A.-M. Bathmaker & P. Harnett (Eds.), *Exploring Learning Identity and Power through Life History and Narrative Research* (pp. 97–111). London: Routledge.

Spivak, C. G. (1999). *Can the Subaltern Speak?* Cambridge, MA: Harvard University Press.

Steinburg, S. R. (2020). Say What, Sisyphus? Decolonising Our Attempts and Decolonisation. In M. L. Moncrieffe, R. Race, & R. Harris (Eds.), *Decolonising the Curriculum – Transnational Perspectives, Research Intelligence Issue 142, Spring 2020* (p. 26). London: British Educational Research Association. https://www.bera.ac.uk/publication/spring-2020.

Tomlinson, S. (2005). Race, Ethnicity and Education Under New Labour. *Oxford Review of Education, 31*(1), 153–171. https://doi.org/10.1080/0305498042000337246.

Traille, K. (2007). 'You Should be Proud About Your History. They Made Me Feel Ashamed:' Teaching History Hurts. *Teaching History, 127*, 6–9.

CHAPTER 2

'Epistemic Violence' in the History Curriculum

Abstract This chapter opens with a brief discussion on the inquiry into the murder of the Black-British teenager Stephen Lawrence in 1993, and the 7/7 terrorist attacks in London in 2005. This is to give a sense of how the British government have responded to cross-cultural racial encounters through curriculum design for teaching and learning in schools about British history and nationhood. Following this, the focus is set on understanding why a shift to Neo-Conservative ideologies seen though a White-British 'master narrative' has been reasserted today as a dominant educational discourse of the history curriculum. The impact of this ideological approach to teaching and learning on non-White pupils is argued as 'epistemic violence'.

Keywords Our Island Story • Master narrative • Neo-conservatism • Epistemic violence

Teaching and Learning Interests

In being a Black-British born man, an educator and a former primary school teacher with African-Caribbean roots and heritage stemming from mass-migration and settlement to the British Isles after World War Two, I am particularly concerned with exploring and understanding societal issues, political and educational discourses in relation to my minority-ethnic group in Britain. For example, the inquiry into the

© The Author(s) 2020
M. L. Moncrieffe, *Decolonising the History Curriculum*,
https://doi.org/10.1007/978-3-030-57945-6_2

racially motivated murder of Black-British teenager Stephen Lawrence in London, in 1993 by a White-British gang of young men.[1] Arresting and bringing these murderers to court to face justice became a major ordeal for Stephen's parents during a period of time in Britain when the Conservative government was in power (Egwuonwu 2019; Heal 2018; Cathcart 2000). In fact, it was four years before an official public inquiry on the murder of Stephen was began. This inquiry was commissioned by the newly elected New Labour Government in 1997. The MacPherson report (1999) into Stephen's murder arrived two years later. This exposed London Metropolitan Police failings rooted to White-British institutional racism. MacPherson (1999) spoke to the need for transforming education in society about race-equality; cultural diversity and cultural differences (Race 2015, 2019). This is something that I agreed with. Furthermore, I believed that primary school teaching and learning through a decolonised history curriculum could support MacPherson's (1999) recommendations.

Following the 7/7 London terrorist attacks in 2005,[2] contemporary British multiculturalism was identified and blamed for being the root cause of these attacks (Race 2015). Political discourses emerged calling for new approaches to education and curriculum content for teaching and learning about British history, culture, identity formation and nationhood (Straw 2007; Brown 2006). Former school headteacher Keith Ajegbo et al. (2007) reported to the New Labour government, and recommended an approach to curriculum teaching and learning that sought to advance notions of citizenship and diversity through an in-depth exploration of personal histories and notions of 'Britishness'. It was an approach to the study of British history that I agreed with. However, Ajegbo et al.'s (2007) recommendation was abandoned in 2010 by the Conservative/Liberal Democrat coalition government educational ideology for curriculum teaching and learning of British history in the primary school.

[1] Stephen Lawrence (13 September 1974–22 April 1993) a Black-British teenager from Plumstead, South-East London was murdered in a racially motivated attack while waiting for a bus in Well Hall, Eltham on the evening of 22nd April 1993.
[2] The 7th July 2005 London bombings, often referred to as 7/7, were a series of coordinated terrorist suicide attacks in London.

Reasserting 'Our Island Story'

> The current approach we have - denies children the opportunity to hear our island story. Well, this trashing of our past has to stop (Gove 2010).

In 2010, the Conservative politician Michael Gove became the Secretary of State for Education. His criticism of the 'current approach' to thinking pointed to Ajegbo et al. (2007). Gove (2010) stated a desire to reset the national history curriculum for teaching and learning in schools, in a bid to apply a chronological approach for telling the story of Britain's past (from the Stone Ages to beginning the twentieth century) similar to the shape and contents of *Our Island Story* (1905/2005). This is a book written by Henrietta Marshall, first published in the year 1905,[3] at the pinnacle of British Empire power in its imperial rule of multiple countries across the world. The stories in this book romanticise the White-British past through the lives of kings, queens, folk heroes, and heroines all of which are which are considered as central to the myth of British history (Nichol and Harnett 2011). *Our Island Story* (1905/2005) was approved by the British government's Board of Education in 1904 as a 'master narrative' of British history (Evans 2011; Nichol and Harnett 2011) spoken through a Neo-conservative 'traditionalist' viewpoint (Bartlett and Burton 2016; Matheson 2016). The stories in *Our Island Story* (1905/2005) maintain in the present and for the future a 'narcissistic' White-British perspective with national history, identity and nationhood (Bartlett and Burton 2016; Matheson 2016). In describing this, Samuel (2003, p. 82) writes: 'For Conservatives… nation is primordial, a transcendent unity of time and space which connects the living and the dead with the yet unborn.'

Nichol and Harnett (2011) reported on how primary school history teachers articulated their worries on the lack of teaching and learning direction and guidance that would help them to engage pupils in their classrooms with more diverse and multicultural perspectives of British history. This raises a concern about Gove's (2010) Neo-conservative ideology for history education in schools. The Key Stage 2 primary school history curriculum (DfE 2013a) is framed by a narrow White-British only

---

[3] *Our Island Story* (1905) was republished in 2005 by The Study of Civil Society (CIVITAS), a conservative-right organisation, with support from the *The Daily Telegraph*. This enabled free copies of the book to be distributed to schools across England (See Chap. 3)

perspective, and as 'master narrative' for curriculum teaching and learning it gives no other direction or guidance for alternative routes of knowing about British history.

Competing Discourses on History Education

The curriculum is argued as being the pre-eminent issue in education (Young 2014). What it means to think historically about the story of Britain's past is the central theme to an ongoing conflict between two opposing discourses on the purpose and function of history education (Harris and Reynolds 2014). Professional discourses have generally viewed and approached the story of Britain's past through historical enquiry with a lens of uncertainty; seeing teaching and learning of the subject framed by openness and fluidity in thinking (Brokenhurst and Phillips 2004; Low-Beer 2003; Phillips 1992, 1999, 2003; Alibhai-Brown 2000; Price 1968). On the other hand, Public discourses (where Neo-conservative ideology is positioned) sees the function of history education as being to prioritise an acquisition of the historical record based upon core knowledge; seeing teaching and learning of the subject more factually and with closure and stricture (Phillips 1999). This is a view that the purpose for history education in schools is as a vehicle for disseminating stories and traditions as a 'master narrative' (Harris 2020; Nichol and Harnett 2011). This is where students can learn traditional 'facts' about the nation's past, and teaching learning via the history curriculum supports the maintenance of cultural hegemony (Gramsci 1971, 2012).

Teaching and Learning About Mass-Migration

In my own critical thinking about the Key Stage 2 primary school history curriculum, I examined its 'Purpose of Study' and the knowledge offered through its aims and contents, and in relation to teaching and learning about mass-migration and settlement to the British Isles over the ages. This is because I was interested in knowing how I could transform my classroom teaching and learning on race-equality; cultural diversity and cultural differences through history, and in relation to recommendations from Macpherson (1999). The 'Purpose of Study' for the entire history curriculum (DfE 2013a, b) speaks of helping 'pupils gain a coherent knowledge and understanding of Britain's past' and helping 'pupils to understand the complexity of people's lives, the process of change, the diversity of societies and relationships between different groups, as well as their own identity'

(DfE 2013a, p. 1). However, at Key Stage 2 the historical journey in the 'Purpose of Study' is shaped by 'statutory' directives for teaching and learning through Eurocentric experiences only. These are: 'Britain's settlement by Anglo Saxons and Scots'; 'Viking and Anglo-Saxon struggle', and by explicit guidance to include the 'Scots invasions'; 'Anglo Saxon invasions, settlements', 'Viking raids and invasion' (DfE 2013a, p. 4). The sense emerging from this is that pupils understanding about 'nation building' and 'national identity' are to arrive specifically through learning only about those Eurocentric moments from the past. The national curriculum chronology for teaching and learning British history in Key Stage 2 history stops at the year 1066. This means that over 950 years of chronological mass-migration and settlement history since the year 1066 is missing. There is no explicit unit of study in the aims or contents of the Key Stage 2 primary school history curriculum that speaks directly to teachers developing pupils learning about 'nation building' and 'national identity' through the lives and experiences of non-White settlers on the British Isles over the ages. It seems fair to acknowledge that non-White settlers and migrant groups over different periods in history, have added their different values to the cultural mix on the British Isles (Race 2015). A broader approach to this study could perhaps relate to what the 'Purpose of Study' suggests by helping 'pupils to understand the complexity of people's lives, the process of change, the diversity of societies and relationships between different groups, as well as their own identity' (DfE 2013a, p. 1).

WHITE-ONLY CURRICULUM DIRECTION AND GUIDANCE

There may appear to be some scope for the primary school teacher to think about 'the diversity of societies and relationships between different groups.' This comes through the statutory unit of teaching and learning: 'a study of an aspect or theme in British history that extends pupils' chronological knowledge beyond 1066' (DfE 2013a, p. 5). However, this unit of study raises a concern, where its 'non-statutory' guidance speaks to the centricity of Eurocentric lives experiences and histories:

- the changing power of monarchs using case studies such as John, Anne, and Victoria
- changes in an aspect of social history, such as crime and punishment from the Anglo-Saxons to the present or leisure and entertainment in the twentieth Century

- the legacy of Greek or Roman culture (art, architecture, or literature) on later periods in British history, including the present day
- a significant turning point in British history, for example, the first railways or the Battle of Britain

In all 'statutory directives', and 'non-statutory' guidance, the Key Stage 2 primary school history curriculum is framed by the lives and experiences of European ethnic and cultural groups of people from past, who by their ethnogenesis (Harke 1998, 2011) are most likely to related to current White-British ethnic majority population. White only curriculum direction and guidance dominates the aims and contents of the Key Stage 2 primary school history curriculum. This has the potential to suffocate the opportunity for thinking about teaching and learning the story of Britain's past through non-White multicultural British histories.

Looking Beyond Key Stage 2

I discovered what I interpreted as a clearer teaching and learning statement on mass-migration and settlement to the British Isles when looking beyond the Key Stage 2 primary school history curriculum to secondary education and the 'History programmes of study: Key Stage 3' (students aged 11 to 14 years old) (DfE 2013b):

> a study of an aspect of social history, such as the impact through time of the migration of people to, from and within the British Isles' (DfE 2013b, p. 5).

It appears that the inclusion of multicultural British histories could be covered in classroom teaching and learning (Macintosh et al. 2019). But, why should all pupils have to wait until they enter Key Stage 3 education to be taught about the broader histories of British multicultural diversity beyond that of Eurocentrism? In fact, this opportunity for education and learning may not even occur. This is because the Key Stage 3 curriculum statement is 'non-statutory' guidance. Therefore, secondary schools and Key Stage 3 teachers of history are neither obliged to, nor held to account on whether or not they teach their students 'the impact through time of the migration of people to, from and within the British Isles' (DfE 2013b, p. 5). However, Key Stage 2 primary school teachers are fully obligated by the Key Stage 2 history curriculum 'statutory' directives to teach pupils about the arrival to the British Isles of Saxons and Vikings from mainland Europe.

Absence of a Black-British Presence

There was before the current Key Stage 2 history curriculum (DfE 2013a) a greater possibility for Key Stage 2 pupils to study a wider representation of mass-migration and settlement to the British Isles. Guidance came through an associated scheme of work exemplar: 'Unit 13: How has life in Britain Changed Since 1948' (DfEE 1999; QCA 1998). With this, primary school teachers could place emphasis on pupils learning through the experiences of a wider variety of ethnic and cultural groups who had settled in post-World War Two Britain. Despite this, Gardner (2001) in his search for a multicultural curriculum asserted that a large body of knowledge on Black-British history was very much absent from the history of Britain taught in schools. Mass-migration and settlement to the British Isles by minority-ethnic groups from Africa and Asia, and from across the world was already occurring way before the year 1948 (Adi 2019; Olusoga 2016; Winder 2013; Miles 2005).

'Epistemic Violence'

Despite various iterations of the national curriculum for history, little has changed, and the framework of knowledge for the history curriculum remains Eurocentric, male and White, inward-looking and regressive (Harris 2020; Alexander et al. 2015; Kapoor 2013; Osler 2009; Gillborn 2008; Tomlinson 2005). This aims and contents of the national history curriculum through its various iterations has served to cause disengagement with minority-ethnic group pupils, where they fail to sense any connection and belonging to its view of British history (Charles 2019; Harris and Reynolds 2014; Hawkey and Prior 2011; Smart 2010; Maylor et al. 2007). Traille (2007, p. 32) discusses students of African-Caribbean heritage in their learning of history as 'implicitly and explicitly negatively stereotyped by teachers and peers' through identities imposed on Black people in the past that they rejected. Grever et al. (2008) speak of minority-ethnic students in their learning of school history becoming disengaged and being at odds with conceptions of their identity expressed in nationalistic terms, which can develop and sustain a crisis of identity in association to their history and their birthplace. This Eurocentric curriculum content inflicts "epistemic violence" (Chakravorty Spivak 1999) on non-White British children, by imposing an authoritative view on how to see the world in the past, present and future.

References

Adi, H. (Ed.). (2019). *Black British History: New Perspectives*. London: Zed Books.

Ajegbo, K., Kiwan, D., & Sharma, S. (2007). *Curriculum, Diversity & Citizenship*. Nottingham: DfES. Retrieved October 2, 2016, from http://www.educationengland.org.uk/documents/pdfs/2007-ajegbo-report-citizenship.pdf

Alexander, C., Weekes-Bernard, D., & Chatterji, J. (2015). *History Lessons: Teaching Diversity In and Through the History National Curriculum*. London: Runnymede.

Alibhai-Brown, Y. (2000). *Who Do We Think We Are? Imagining the New Britain*. London: Penguin.

Bartlett, S., & Burton, D. (2016). *Introduction to Education Studies* (4th ed.). London: Sage.

Brokenhurst, H., & Phillips, R. (Eds.). (2004). *History, Nationhood and the Question of Britain*. Basingstoke: Palgrave Macmillan.

Brown, G. (2006). *Who Do We Want to Be? The Future of Britishness*. Speech given to the Fabian Society, 16th January 2006. Retrieved August 6, 2014, from http://fabians.org.uk/events/new-year-conference-06/brown-britishness/speech

Cathcart, B. (2000). *The Case of Stephen Lawrence*. London: Penguin Books.

Charles, M. (2019). Effective Teaching and Learning: Decolonizing the Curriculum. *Journal of Black Studies*, 50(8), 731–766. https://doi.org/10.1177/0021934719885631.

Departement of Education and Employment (DfEE). (1999). *The National Curriculum: Handbook for Primary Teachers in England*. www.nc.uk.net. Key Stages 1 and 2. Retrieved September 13, 2016, from http://webarchive.nationalarchives.gov.uk/20130401151715/http://www.education.gov.uk/publications/eOrderingDownload/QCA-99-457.pdf

Department for Education (DfE). (2013a, July). 'History Programmes of Study: Key Stages 1 and 2'. National Curriculum in England. In *The National Curriculum in Britain Framework Document*. London: DfE.

Department for Education (DfE). (2013b, July). 'History Programmes of Study: Key Stages 3 and 4'. National Curriculum in England. In *The National Curriculum in Britain Framework Document*. London: DfE.

Egwuonwu, B. (2019). *Twenty Years on from the Inquiry into Stephen Lawrence's Racist Murder – What's Changed?* Retrieved April 5, 2019, from https://eachother.org.uk/twenty-years-on-from-the-inquiry-into-stephen-lawrences-racist-murder-whats-changed/

Evans, R. J. (2011). The Wonderfulness of Us. *London: Review of Book*, 33(6), 9–12.

Gardner, P. (2001). *Teaching and Learning in Multicultural Classrooms*. London: David Fulton Publishers.

Gillborn, D. (2008). *Racism and education: Coincidence or conspiracy?* London: Routledge.

Gove, M. (2010). *All pupils will learn our island story.* Speech at Conservative Party Conference, Birmingham. Retrieved August 6, 2014, from http://centrallobby.politicshome.com/latestnews/article-detail/newsarticle/speech-in-full-michael-gove/

Gramsci, A. (1971). *Selections from Prison Notebooks.* London: Lawrence and Wishart.

Gramsci, A. (2012). *Selections from Cultural Writings.* London: Lawrence & Wishart Limited.

Grever, M., Haydn, T., & Ribbens, K. (2008). Identity and School History: The Perspective of Young People from the Netherlands and Britain. *British Journal of Educational Studies,* 56(1), 76–94. https://doi.org/10.1111/j.1467-8527.2008.00396.x.

Harke, H. (1998). Archaeologists and Migration: A Problem of Attitude. *Current Archaeology,* 39, 19–45. https://doi.org/10.1086/204697.

Harke, H. (2011). Anglo Saxon Immigration and Ethnogenesis. *Medieval Archaeology,* 55, 1–28. https://doi.org/10.1179/174581711X13103897378311.

Harris, R. (2020). Decolonising the History Curriculum. In M. L. Moncrieffe, R. Race, & R. Harris (Eds.), *Decolonising the Curriculum – Transnational Perspectives, Research Intelligence Issue 142, Spring 2020* (p. 16). London: British Educational Research Association. https://www.bera.ac.uk/publication/spring-2020.

Harris, R., & Reynolds, R. (2014). The History Curriculum and Its Personal Connection to Students from Minority-Ethnic Backgrounds. *Journal of Curriculum Studies,* 46(4), 464–486. https://doi.org/10.1080/00220272.2014.881925.

Hawkey, K., & Prior, J. (2011). History, Memory Cultures and Meaning in the Classroom. *Journal of Curriculum Studies,* 43(2), 231–247. https://doi.org/10.1080/00220272.2010.516022.

Heal, A. (2018). *Stephen Lawrence: Timeline of Key Events.* Retrieved April 4, 2019, from https://www.theguardian.com/uk-news/2018/apr/19/stephen-lawrence-timeline-of-key-events

Kapoor, N. (2013). The Advancement of Racial Neoliberalism in Britain. *Ethnic and Racial Studies,* 36(6), 1028–1046. https://doi.org/10.1080/01419870.2011.629002.

Low-Beer, A. (2003). School History, National History and the Issue of National Identity. *International Journal of Historical Teaching, Learning and Research,* 3(1), 9–14. https://www.ingentaconnect.com/content/ioep/herj/2003/00000003/00000001/art00002.

Macintosh, K., Todd, J., & Das, N. (2019). *Teaching Migration, Belonging, and Empire in Secondary Schools.* London: TIDE-Runnymede.

MacPherson, W. (1999). *The Stephen Lawrence Inquiry: Report of an Inquiry.* London: TSO.

Marshall, H. E. (1905/2005). *Our Island Story*. Galore Park/Civitas: Tenterden and London.
Matheson, D. (Ed.). (2016). *An Introduction to the Study of Education*. Abingdon: Routledge.
Maylor, U., Read, B., Mendick, H., Ross, A., & Rollock, N. (2007). *Diversity and Citizenship in the Curriculum: Research Review*. London: The Institute for Policy Studies in Education London Metropolitan University.
Miles, D. (2005). *The Tribes of Britain: Who Are We? And Where Do We Come From?* London: Weidenfield & Nicolson.
Nichol, J., & Harnett, P. (2011). History Teaching in Britain and British National History Curriculum, Past Present and into the Future. *International Journal of History Learning, Teaching and Research, 10*(1), 106–119.
Olusoga, D. (2016). *Black and British: A Forgotten History*. London: Pan Macmillan.
Osler, A. (2009). Patriotism, Multiculturalism and Belonging: Political Discourse and the Teaching of History. *Educational Review, 61*(1), 85–100. https://doi.org/10.1080/00131910802684813.
Phillips, R. (1992). The Battle for the 'Big Prize': The Creation of Synthesis and the Role of a Curriculum Pressure Group: The Case of History and the National Curriculum. *The Curriculum Journal, 3*(3), 245–260. https://doi.org/10.1080/0958517920030304?journalCode=rcjo20.
Phillips, R. (1999). History Teaching, Nationhood and Politics in England and Wales in the Late 20th Century. *History of Education, 28*(3), 351–363. https://doi.org/10.1080/004676099284672?journalCode=thed20.
Phillips, R. (2003). British Island Stories: History, Schools and Nationhood. *International Journal of Historical Teaching, Learning and Research, 3*(1), 3–7.
Price, M. (1968). History in Danger. *History, 53*, 342–347. https://www.jstor.org/stable/24406366.
Qualifications and Curriculum Authority (QCA). (1998). *Unit 13: How has Life in Britain Changed Since 1948*. London: QCA.
Race, R. (2015). *Multiculturalism and Education* (2nd ed.). London: Bloomsbury.
Race, R. (2019). Promoting and Advancing Multicultural Dialogues in Education. *Journal of Dialogue Studies, 6*, 65–71.
Samuel, R. (2003). A Case for National History. *International Journal of Historical Teaching, Learning and Research, 3*(1), 69–73. www.ingentaconnect.com/contentone/ioep/herj/2003/00000003/00000001/art00010.
Smart, D. (2010). Going to the Pictures: Learning to See the Life Stories of Minorities Within Majority Narratives. In A.-M. Bathmaker & P. Harnett (Eds.), *Exploring Learning Identity and Power through Life History and Narrative Research* (pp. 97–111). London: Routledge.
Spivak, G. C. (1999). *Can the Subaltern Speak?* Cambridge: Harvard University Press.

Straw, J. (2007, April 29). We Need a British Story. *The Sunday Times*. Retrieved August 6, 2014, from http://timesonline.co.uk/tol/comment/columnists/guest_contributors/article1720349.ece

Tomlinson, S. (2005). Race, Ethnicity, and Education Under New Labour. *Oxford Review of Education, 31*(1), 153–171. https://doi.org/10.1080/0305498042000337246.

Traille, K. (2007). 'You Should be Proud About Your History. They Made Me Feel Ashamed:' Teaching History Hurts. *Teaching History, 127*, 6–9.

Winder, R. (2013). *Bloody Foreigners: The Story of Immigration to Britain*. London: Abacus.

Young, M. (2014). What Is a Curriculum and What Can It Do? *Curriculum Journal, 25*(1), 7–13. https://doi.org/10.1080/09585176.2014.902526?journalCode=rcjo20.

CHAPTER 3

White Trainee-Teachers Reproduce Eurocentric and White-British Histories

Abstract This chapter applies the theory of 'Whiteness' to examine the aims and contents the Key Stage 2 primary school history curriculum (Department for Education, 'History programmes of study: key stages 1 and 2'. National curriculum in England, In: The national curriculum in Britain framework document. DfE, London, 2013). A discussion is presented on how 'Whiteness' as a cultural belief of supremacy seen in the story of Britain's past has been given political endorsement in the present. 'Whiteness' as the central perspective of the national history curriculum 'Purpose of Study', aims and contents can be reproduced socially as cultural hegemony. White-British trainee-teachers of Key Stage 2 primary school history were asked: What does British history mean to you? Their background histories, experiences of socialisation and their responses to the question indicate that the biggest challenge to decolonising the primary school history curriculum through teaching and learning may be in attempting to reframe Eurocentric mindsets; the default position from which trainee-teachers of White-British mono-ethnic background and socialisation begin to think about teaching the story of Britain's past.

Keywords Whiteness • White privilege • Cultural hegemony • Socialisation • Cultural reproduction

The Default Perspective

Society's default perspective for history is framed by the majoritarian ethnic group, and in Britain that is the privileged 'White' perspective (Harris 2020; Bhopal 2018). White people are taught to see their perspectives as objective and representative of reality, allowing them to view themselves as universal human beings who can represent all of human experience (Di Angelo 2011). It is a standpoint of White privilege—a place from which to view the world—a norm against which the other is judged (Delgado and Stefanic 2012; Gillborn 2008; Ladson-Billings 1998; McIntyre 1997; Frankenburg 1993). Perhaps then, the biggest challenge to decolonising the curriculum is in attempting to reframe a Eurocentric mindset held by the majority of White-British teachers; the default position from which they begin to think about teaching the story of Britain's past. Harris (2020) discusses the need for White-British teachers of history to address their inherited 'White privilege' to focus more on the nature of history i.e. the study of history as a discipline, rather than it being used in schools via curriculum for the inculcation of Eurocentric and White-British propagandas. These ubiquitous and privileged communications are clear and apparent in the Key Stage 2 primary school history curriculum.

Eurocentric and White-British Only Histories

When looking for evidence of the potential to teach and learn about mass-migration and settlement to the British Isles over the ages in the Key Stage 2 primary school history curriculum, the focus provided is on 'conquests', 'invasions' and migration to the British Isles by Roman leaders from Europe and their armies e.g. 'the Roman Empire by AD 42 and the power of its army' and 'successful invasion by Claudius and conquest' (DfE 2013, p. 4). The 'aims' of the Key Stage 2 primary school history curriculum direct attention on migration to the British Isles by Saxon tribes and Viking invaders from mainland Europe i.e. 'Britain's settlement by Anglo-Saxons'; 'Scots invasions from Ireland to north Britain (now Scotland)'; 'Anglo-Saxon invasions, settlements' (DfE 2013, p. 4). This dominance of Eurocentrism represents 'White narcissism' discussed in Chap. 1. Harris (2013) has argued that the past is inherently diverse, so the curriculum should reflect that. African and Asian presence in Roman Britain through the civil and military leadership of Septimius Severus and Quintus Lollius Urbicus is highly documented, and called on for greater use in the national curriculum for history (Adi 2019; Olusoga 2016). Still, there are no clear and explicit aims and contents in relation to the history of cultural diversity on the British Isles over the ages in the Key Stage 2 primary school history curriculum statements. Are the Key Stage 2 national curriculum for history aims and contents racist? A definition of racism is:

> [...] encompassing economic, political, social, and cultural structures, actions, and beliefs that systematize and perpetuate an unequal distribution of privileges, resources and power between White people and people of color (Black people). *This unequal distribution benefits Whites and disadvantages people of color overall, and as a group* (Di Angelo 2011, p. 56).

The Eurocentric and White only depictions of mass-migration and settlement to the British Isles in the Key Stage 2 primary school history curriculum is a dimension of racism that elevates White people over people of colour (Di Angelo 2011). The Key Stage 2 primary school history curriculum is an exclusive route of study that all pupils must endure, looking at lives and experiences of Anglo-Saxons, Vikings and Scots. These are European groups of people from the distant past who through their ethnogenesis (Harke 1998, 2011) are likely to relate to White-British teachers and White-British pupils, more so than any other ethnic groups in society today (Winder 2013; Miles 2005). They are privileged in their teaching and learning. Their sense of connection to this narrative is likely to be stronger than that of non-White primary school teachers and non-White primary school pupils.

WHITENESS OF THE PAST ENDORSED IN THE PRESENT

The amplification of 'Whiteness' as a hegemonic normality (Bhabha 2004) for transmitting the narrative of British history in schools can be identified by the actions of the Institute For The Study Of Civil Society (CIVITAS), a conservative-right organisation. In 2005 it republished Henrietta Marshall's *Our Island Story* (first published in 1905) a celebratory version of Eurocentric and White-British history. CIVITAS said:

> It has become possible to donate free copies of *Our Island Story* to UK schools. ...We hope this will this assist teachers who want to teach narrative history in schools (CIVITAS 2015).

However, the *Our Island Story* (1905/2005) White-British perspective of cross-cultural 'encounters' with peoples across the world presents a White-British cultural superiority over 'other' people. One of many examples in *Our Island Story* (1905/2005) portrays the Maori people as cannibals with a need to be taught and 'civilised' by the White-British through Christianity:

> For many years now White people settled in New Zealand, for it was inhabited by a wild and warlike people called Maori. These Maori were cannibals, that is, people who eat other human beings. After a battle, those who were killed would be roasted and eaten by the victors. The Maori fought among themselves, and they fought with the White traders who came from time to time to their shores. Yet a bold missionary called Marsden, hearing about these islands and their people, made up his mind to try to teach them to be Christian (Marshall 1905/2005, p. 478).

The White-British perspective is a derogatory 'other' view of different ethnicities and cultures to their own. This can be understood through Said's (1978) presentation of the 'occident', a European colonial power world view of nations, cultures, and ethnicities that exist outside their own as being inferiors on the margins, the 'orient'.

It must be remembered that *Our Island Story* (1905/2005) was additionally hailed by David Cameron the Conservative coalition government Prime Minster 2010–2015 where he said:

> When I was younger, I particularly enjoyed *Our Island Story* by Henrietta Elizabeth Marshall. It is written in a way that really captured my imagination and which nurtured my interest in the history of our great nation (Hough 2010).

David Cameron's endorsement of *Our Island Story* (1905/2005) is supportive of White-British cultural beliefs from the past. To what extent do these beliefs remain in the present, and for the future? Hobsbawn (1959, p. 50) reminds us that 'the standard example of an identity culture which anchors itself to the past by means of myths dressed up as history is nationalism'. The stories in *Our Island Story* (1905/2005) include those of crusades to the holy land, and of British colonialism for constructing it's British Empire. *Our Island Story* (1905/2005) is a celebratory version of White-British history that can function to maintain a hegemonic normality (Bhabha 2004) of 'Whiteness'. This version of history aims to reinforce a superior White-British culture and world view, where 'White' becomes the norm from which other 'races' stand apart and in relation to which they are defined' (Gillborn 2008, p. 169). Cross-cultural encounters in *Our Island Story* (1905/2005) present the non-White person as the subordinate 'other' and as the threat. This double discourse emerging from White-British perspectives of cross-cultural encounters is used to justify and to impose their sense of cultural supremacy (Lander 2014). It is a discourse of 'Whiteness' from the past that can also be related to present, particularly when David

Cameron as British Prime Minister (Cameron 2011) attacked the concept of cross-cultural British multiculturalism, calling it a 'failure'.

WHITENESS, POLICY ENACTMENT AND REPRESENTATION

'Whiteness' is a multidimensional social process functioning at all times and on myriad levels; intrinsically linked by dynamic relations of domination that are historically, socially, politically and culturally produced by White people (Di Angelo 2011). White-British majoritarian priorities via curriculum can become transmitted as a body of cultural knowledge (Smith 2000) in teaching and learning. This means that 'Whiteness' is able to function as the "regime of truth" (Foucault 1980). White-British traditions as 'master narratives' can become reproduced as cultural hegemony (Gramsci 1971, 2012). For example, evidence from research on Key Stage 2 primary school teacher interpretations of fundamental British values (DfE 2014) has shown primary school classrooms wall displays being used as the symbolic reification of 'Whiteness' through exclusive White images and White icons, with pupils being able to absorb these visual communications on a daily basis (Moncrieffe and Moncrieffe 2019).

TEACHER SOCIALISATION AND CULTURAL REPRODUCTION OF WHITENESS

Salili and Hoosain (2001) claim that teachers have their own cultural backgrounds, values, customs, perceptions and prejudices and that those cultural characteristics play an important influential role in teaching situations. McCrum (2010, p. 6) sees that 'beginning history teachers' construct their approaches to pedagogy where family background and lived experiences are significant influences on the teachers' beliefs about the nature and purposes of history. It seems therefore that successful cultural hegemonic reproduction of 'Whiteness' through British history in the primary school classroom is a process that is determined by the teacher's personal interpretation of curriculum aims and contents; their social and cultural backgrounds; and their conscious and unconscious experiences of socialisation. This relates to Bourdieu's concept of *habitus* (Bourdieu 1984, 1993, p. 170) 'a way of thinking that is created and reproduced unconsciously'. Gaventa et al. (2016) support this by arguing that the dispositions held by teachers are shaped both by past events and structures, that influence current practices and condition our very perceptions of these. Mohanty (1994) suggests that the educational site is a political and cultural environment in which teachers and students will either produce, reinforce, recreate, resist and transform ideas about history, culture, identity formation and nationhood. The school-teacher workforce census (DfE 2020) reported 85.9% of all teachers in state-funded schools in England were White British (out of those whose ethnicity was known). 3.9% of teachers were from the White Other ethnic group, the second highest percentage after the White British group. 92.9% of headteachers were White British. Just 2.2% of teachers were Black people. These figures indicate the dominance of White-British teachers in the school population. Could this then mean that they will be more inclined to maintain the cultural reproduction of White-British history for teaching and learning in schools and classrooms? Boronski and Hassan (2015, p. 122) argue:

> [...] if Whites mainly interact with only each other, then this can result in the sharing of similar cultural and racial experiences. This can influence the formulation of shared attitudes, thereby reinforcing their socialisation and the developing 'White socialisation' [...] this allows for further White supremacy ideologies to prevail because in a setting where shared values and attitudes about non-Whites dominate, White privilege becomes invisible.

The pedagogical motives of primary school history teachers concerning their underlying principles and practices are generally guided by their ethnic and social backgrounds in both the conscious and unconscious decisions that they make when interpreting the national curriculum for history (Sossick 2010; Smart 2010; Harnett 2000). Burns (2014) speaks about teachers' 'involved experience' having the capacity to either broaden or narrow the scope and depth of coverage offered during teaching and learning, thus framing the historical outlook of the learner.

Examining Trainee-Teachers' Perceptions

In order to explore the potential of White-British primary school history trainee-teachers reproducing the 'Whiteness' of the Key Stage 2 history curriculum by the influence of their ethnic, cultural and social backgrounds, a semi-structured questionnaire was devised and disseminated across a teacher-training institute. This gained responses from twenty-one primary school history trainee-teachers.

Table 3.1 presents the identities of trainee-teachers. Pseudonyms have been applied. Categorising them via their background experiences allowed

Table 3.1 Identities of trainee-teachers

Name	Gender	Ethnic group	Age group	Neighbourhood as a child and teenager	Ethnic make-up of Primary school	Ethnic make-up of Secondary School	Experience and study of history as a subject
Ann	Female	White-British/Irish	18–25	Generally mono-ethnic White-British	Generally mono-ethnic White-British	Generally mono-ethnic White-British	A level AS level GCSE
Sally	Female	White-British	18–25	Generally mono-ethnic White-British	Generally mono-ethnic White-British	Generally mono-ethnic White-British	A level AS level GCSE
Jo	Female	White-British	18–25	Generally mono-ethnic White-British	Generally mono-ethnic White-British	Generally mono-ethnic White-British	A level
Debbie	Female	White-British	26–32	Generally mono-ethnic White-British	Generally mono-ethnic White-British	Generally mono-ethnic White-British	A level
Diana	Female	White-British	18–25	Generally mono-ethnic White-British	Generally mono-ethnic White-British	Generally mono-ethnic White-British	GCSE
Laura	Female	White-British	18–25	Generally mono-ethnic White-British	Generally mono-ethnic White-British	Generally mono-ethnic White-British	A level
Catherine	Female	White-British	18–25	Generally mono-ethnic White-British	Generally mono-ethnic White-British	Generally mono-ethnic White-British	GCSE AS level A level

(*continued*)

Table 3.1 (continued)

Name	Gender	Ethnic group	Age group	Neighbourhood as a child and teenager	Ethnic make-up of Primary school	Ethnic make-up of Secondary School	Experience and study of history as a subject
James	Male	White-British	26–32	Generally mono-ethnic White-British	Generally mono-ethnic White-British	Generally mono-ethnic White-British	A level
Victoria	Female	White-British	18–25	Generally mono-ethnic White-British	Generally mono-ethnic White-British	Generally mono-ethnic White-British	A level
Tom	Male	White-British	18–25	Generally mono-ethnic White-British	Generally mono-ethnic White-British	Generally multi-ethnic	GCSE
Dawn	Female	White-British	18–25	Generally mono-ethnic White-British	Generally mono-ethnic White-British	Generally mono-ethnic White-British	A level
Chloe	Female	White-British	18–25	Generally mono-ethnic White-British	Generally mono-ethnic White-British	Generally mono-ethnic White-British	A level
Olivia	Female	White-British	18–25	Generally multi-ethnic	Generally mono-ethnic White-British	Generally multi-ethnic	AS level GCSE
Rachel	Female	White-British	26–32	Generally multi-ethnic	Generally multi-ethnic	Generally multi-ethnic	AS level GCSE
Billie	Female	White-other	18–25	Generally multi-ethnic	Generally multi-ethnic	Generally multi-ethnic	None

(*continued*)

Table 3.1 (continued)

Name	Gender	Ethnic group	Age group	Neighbourhood as a child and teenager	Ethnic make-up of Primary school	Ethnic make-up of Secondary School	Experience and study of history as a subject
Emma	Female	White-British	18–25	Generally multi-ethnic	Generally multi-ethnic	Generally multi-ethnic	GSCE
Sasha	Female	No answer	Over 40	Mono-ethnic and multi-ethnic (both)	Generally mono-ethnic White-British	Generally multi-ethnic	GCSE
Holly	Female	White-British	26–32	Generally mono-ethnic White-British	Generally mono-ethnic White-British	Generally mono-ethnic White-British	None
Poppy	Female	White-British	18–25	Generally mono-ethnic White-British	Generally mono-ethnic White-British	Generally multi-ethnic	None
Daisy	Female	White-British	26–32	Generally mono-ethnic White-British	Generally mono-ethnic White-British	Generally multi-ethnic	None
Alison	Female	White-British	18–25	Generally mono-ethnic White-British	Mono-ethnic and multi-ethnic (both)	Mono-ethnic and multi-ethnic (both)	None

for a consideration of their socialisation and the potential impact of that on their thoughts about British history.

Follow-up interviews were also conducted with the focus on two key questions:

1. What perceptions do trainee-teachers have of teaching and learning about mass-migration and settlement to the British Isles over the

ages within the aims and contents of the Key Stage 2 history curriculum?
2. To what extent do trainee-teachers identify a culturally diverse perspective of British history within the aims and contents of the Key Stage 2 national history curriculum?

Ethnic Background

Eighteen of the trainee-teachers declared their ethnicity as White-British; one trainee-teacher declared as White British/Irish; one White-Other; one gave no answer. Nineteen declared as female, and two declared as male. A limitation of this sample is that it was unable to test for understanding the potential impact of ethnicity, cultural background and socialisation by Black-British or Asian primary school history trainee-teachers. In fact, the trainee-teacher sample is reflective of the dominant ethnic and gender make up of the school-teacher population i.e. in general being White-British female teachers (DfE 2020). The responses given by the trainee-teachers to the questionnaire enabled the generalising of understanding from the group about how their ethnicity, cultural backgrounds and socialisation can shape the processes of their thinking for teaching and learning about mass-migration and settlement to the British Isles over the ages in relation to the aims and contents of the Key Stage 2 primary school history curriculum.

Neighbourhoods

Sixteen of the trainee-teachers described the neighbourhood that they lived and grew up in as being dominantly White-British and mono-ethnic. Five of the trainee-teachers described their neighbourhood as being ethnically diverse. The locations that they mention are presented as capital letters.

Sally: My neighbourhood I grew up in was mainly White-British with very limited minority ethnic groups.
Jo: I grew up in a working middle class area made up of predominantly White-British citizens.
Debbie: I have, and still live in a neighbourhood which generally consists of a White-British ethnic group.

Chloe: I moved at the age of 16 from an area in H where there were very few ethnic families, to a more deprived area of B. This change in housing brought a bigger mix of ethnic groups, although still largely White-British.

Laura: I'm from N which isn't known to be very multi-ethnic. In my neighbourhood, most children were White-British. There were some Black people, but I don't remember any Chinese or South American people. On my street, I only remember it having White-British people.

Socialisation at Primary School

A similar theme of dominant White-British socialisation is revealed, where seventeen from twenty-one responses declared their attendance as pupils at majority mono-ethnic White-British primary schools.

Jo: It was mainly a school with White-British children in. My class had two Black children and a boy from up north. The only different accent in the school.

Catherine: I was not aware of any children or teachers who were not White-British.

James: The primary school I attended was mainly of a White-British ethnic group.

Tom: Mainly White-British children with a few Black-British and a child of Indian descent.

Debbie: Although there were different ethnic groups there was still a British-White dominance.

Two White-British trainee-teachers declared that they attended multi-ethnic primary schools as pupils. They speak of their socialisation through a broader view of cultural and ethnically diverse people.

Emma: At my primary school there were children from all different backgrounds and cultures. There was a mix of ethnic groups within the school.

Rachel: I had many friends and teachers from different ethnic groups.

Socialisation at Secondary School and Beyond

Twelve of the trainee-teachers declared their education at majority mono-ethnic White-British background secondary schools; eight were educated at a multi-ethnic secondary schools, and one response said 'both'. The responses of trainee-teachers on their experiences of secondary school education denote their awareness of being raised on cultural differences in Britain, through an increase in the ethnic diversity of people around them.

Catherine: Although there was a White-British dominance there was much more of a mixture of ethnic groups. I can only assume the huge increase of size from Primary to Secondary and the catchment area would have shown this reflection.

Laura: Personally, I never met anyone who was not White-British until I came to university. Where I come from there were very few other ethnic groups.

Trainee-teachers educated at multi-ethnic secondary noticed an increase in the ethnic diversity of people around them and therefore their awareness being raised on cultural differences in Britain.

Poppy: Although my secondary school was in the same neighbourhood as my primary, there was a greater mix of ethnic groups.

Rachel: There were around 20+ ethnic backgrounds in our secondary school.

Sasha: A mix of ethnicities—mainly White-British, Black-British, Indian, and Chinese ethnic groups.

Daisy: Despite the majority of pupils still being of White-British ethnicity, there were more pupils of a mixed ethnic group.

Influences on Knowing British History

It is either secondary school education or the following educational site attended that is the seminal space of cross-cultural and cross-ethnic encounters with multi-ethnic Britain, for trainee-teachers of majority mono-ethnic White-British neighbourhoods and mono-ethnic White-British primary school backgrounds. However, it is an experience of multi-ethnic socialisation that appears to have had no clear influence on their thinking about British history and the story of Britain's past. Instead, these trainee-teachers see their influence on thinking about British history through experiences with their parents and family interests.

Dawn: Trips to sites with family and friends such as natural history museum. I spent a lot of my childhood in P, where there are lots of historical sites.

Victoria: I used to spend time visiting museums and places of some historical significance e.g. battlefields in F with family and I loved it.

Catherine: My father would continually tell me of stories of our country and what it and the people have suffered and always emphasised the importance and value of history and how it creates our future. This made me want to know more about the history of different aspects such as war societies.

Holly: I spent most of my childhood visiting castles and historic sites with my parents. Both of my parents are very interested in their History.

Laura: My father had a keen interest that meant a lot of visits and day trips to historical places, castles, battlefields, museums.

Tom: My family's trips to certain places such as B to visit trenches and experience how it might have felt for the soldiers really inspired me.

The responses above suggest that what is valued as history and heritage by the families and parents of the trainee-teachers may also have potential to be reinvested in their practice as stories and events of significance for their teaching and learning about British history. This connects with what McCrum (2010, p. 6) has discussed about 'beginning history teachers'; their family background and lived experiences as being significant influences on the teachers' beliefs about the nature and purposes of history. Interestingly, this transference of historical and cultural knowledge by the parents of trainee-teachers is accepted as nothing but good: 'I loved it'—Victoria. 'It … really inspired me'—Tom. Here are examples of responses that show enthusiasm to the influence on their dispositions in thinking about British history, through themes of 'War' and trips to 'battlefields' and 'castles'; 'stories of our country'; 'visit the trenches'. It appears that these trainee-teachers have experienced an exclusive form of White-British cultural-historical induction, what Williams (1976, p. 80) describes as learning a 'particular way of life, whether of a people, a period, or a group'.

Trainee-teachers of multi-ethnic neighbourhoods and multi-ethnic primary school background also showed no clear influences of their increased secondary school cross-cultural and cross-ethnic encounters as having an impact on their thinking for teaching about the story of Britain's past. The influence of their parents or family members was not considered by them as being significant to their interests in knowing about British history. Instead, they spoke about their own personal interests with learning history and influences from school.

Olivia: I enjoyed visiting historical places—places that hold great importance in my spare time, both within the UK and abroad.

Billie: Teachers and school in general have influenced my enjoyment of the subject History. I enjoyed the topics I learnt about and the school trips.

Teaching the Story of British History

Trainee-teachers of majority mono-ethnic White-British neighbourhoods and mono-ethnic White-British primary school backgrounds speak to an importance to teach about the lives of British Monarchs, World War One and World War Two.

Catherine: I think it's important for children to learn about monarchs and key eras say like the Victorian era, erm… like Henry the Eighth; Queen Victoria, stuff like that. Henry the Eighth sticks out because… he was quite an interesting one to learn about.'

Anne: What springs to mind only because I am doing it for my history at the moment is World War One […] So I think obviously the World Wars did have a big impact on how this country is, so were important. You could do the Royal Family… that's quite… interesting. Erm, when it comes to migration and stuff, I remember learning about the potato famine and all the Irish going to England and America. But I don't know if that would be… like I said you would need to try and see who was in your class and maybe try and make it relevant to them.

This response given by Anne is interesting. She thinks briefly on her own learning and knowledge which is fed by her ethnic and cultural background in being White-British/Irish. Her background, education and socialisation has some influence on her initial dispositions for thinking about British history and the story of Britain's past being led from a White-British/Irish perspective. However, she questions that thinking and pauses: 'But I don't know if that would be…' She reconsiders the value of teaching and learning about the 'potato famine' by saying that it would only be relevant to who was in the classroom for telling that story of British history. This shows Anne shutting down the initial passion of her ethnic and cultural dispositions with British history.

Trainee-teachers of multi-ethnic neighbourhoods and multi-ethnic primary school backgrounds speak to an importance to teach about the story of British people including ethnic and cultural developments from the past to the present.

Emma: British history to me means all of the significant events which took place from the past and the present in order to form the way we are today. For example, the mix of cultures over the years has widened foods etc. available to us.
Billie: British history to me is how this country has developed and been influenced in order to make it how it is today.
Rachel: British history encompasses the origin of the islands. British history should focus on people, society, right up to the present day.

Teaching About Mass Migration and Settlement

Trainee-teachers of majority mono-ethnic White-British neighbourhoods and mono-ethnic White-British primary school backgrounds relate teaching the story of British history through mass-migration and settlement concerning the Romans, the Anglo Saxons and the Vikings.

James: Migration could be incorporated into the teaching of Britain's settlement by Anglo Saxons and the Scots, as well as the Viking invasions.

Catherine: The first thing I think of is like Anglo Saxons and Romans, like the roads; the baths. Settlements, like the first people to settle came from somewhere else and that's how Britain came about kind of thing.

Victoria: Saxons, Romans, Vikings.

Dawn: In the early studies of history: Romans, Anglo-Saxons, relate to migration.

These trainee-teachers do not think for teaching about the broader ethnic diversity of mass-migration and settlement of Romans to the British Isles (Adi 2019; Olusoga 2016; Weekes-Bernard 2013). This came as a surprise, given that they all studied History at Advanced Level. Still, they also did not discuss specifically any White European leaders of the Romans on the British Isles such as Claudius. However, in their thinking about teaching and learning the history of mass-migration and settlement to the British Isles, they all positioned with the 'Saxons' and 'Vikings'. It shows their orientation with Eurocentric stories from the past to fit the theme of mass-migration and settlement. This is a Eurocentric mindset to show White-British trainee-teachers of majority mono-ethnic White-British neighbourhoods and mono-ethnic White-British primary school backgrounds being fully aligned with the aims and contents of the Key Stage 2 primary school history curriculum. This points to the likelihood of reproduction and maintenance of cultural hegemony (Gramsci 1971, 2012) in their teaching about mass-migration and settlement to the British Isles.

The pattern of thinking from trainee-teachers of multi-ethnic neighbourhoods and multi-ethnic primary school backgrounds speak to exploring diversity of people the past in relation to present and of seeing history in relation to personal and family stories.

Rachel: The movement of people and range of people that have inhabited Britain. How they have helped to shape what our country—and countries—are today. The story of Britain, the story of people, the stories of each child that we teach including personal histories of the children we teach: Where are their families from? How has this shaped them as a person? What significant events have happened in their lifetime.

Emma: Children can relate to migration more when it is introduced as a theme of how Britain came to be what it is today through a variety of aspects.

The views of Rachel and Emma relate to Runnymede (2012) *Making Histories*. This seeks to connect personal histories for demonstrating to all pupils the ways that migration as concept and historical process has impacted on the lives and experiences of all individuals living in modern Britain (Runnymede Trust 2012).

Teaching the History of Ethnic and Cultural Diversity in Britain

When the idea about teaching the history of ethnic and cultural diversity in Britain through the story of mass-migration and settlement was planted in their minds of trainee-teachers of majority mono-ethnic White-British neighbourhoods and mono-ethnic White-British primary school backgrounds, some became open to the possibilities. For example:

Catherine: Like we are like a multi-ethnic… culture which… like the diversity of this should be valued I think and… everything should be respected like you know… so I would want to put that in the classroom. I think that it is quite important to value that multi-ethnic culture.

Unfortunately, Catherine nor any of the other teachers could provide examples of how they would aim to implement this. Interestingly, trainee-teachers of multi-ethnic neighbourhoods and multi-ethnic primary school backgrounds appeared to require less probing for identifying the possibility of teaching and learning via ethnic and culturally diverse perspectives of British history.

Rachel: Britain is a multicultural society and thus children will learn about migration and how it has impacted on Britain and therefore, how this has impacted on the wider world. Recent migration could be looked at and how it influences life in Britain.

Emma: One that stands out to me is the initial aim as it enables children to relate to migration more as it introduced the theme of how Britain come to be what it is today through a variety of aspects.

The Biggest Challenge

The majority of trainee teachers in this sample were of White-British mono-ethnic background and socialisation. The dominant themes from their responses to the semi-structured questionnaire and in their interviews provide evidence of their natural orientations to think about teaching and learning British history from a Eurocentric and White-British perspective. This is a positioning that aligns with aims and contents of the Key Stage 2 primary school history curriculum. A smaller group of teachers in this sample were White-British trainee-teachers of multi-ethnic backgrounds and socialisation. They were able to think about British history and see the possibilities of teaching and learning from ethnically and culturally diverse multicultural perspectives, giving some sense of 'epistemic innovation' (Domínguez 2019) in their thoughts for future practice. The trainee-teachers of White-British mono-ethnic backgrounds and socialisation are influenced by the historical knowledge of Britain imparted to them through their parents and families. These trainee-teachers have learned and discovered about British history through stories of wars, castles, battlefields, military sites, and visits to the trenches. They spoke to a significance of the British Monarchy for teaching and learning the story of Britain's past. They spoke to a significance of the Romans, Anglo-Saxons and Vikings for pupils learning about mass-migration and settlement to the British Isles. Through these Eurocentric lenses of British history, they articulate from a standpoint of White privilege—a place from which to view the world—a norm against which the other is judged (Delgado and Stefanic 2012; Gillborn 2008; Ladson-Billings 1998; McIntyre 1997; Frankenburg 1993). It is a finding that chimes with what was stated at the beginning of this chapter through Harris (2020) concerning the need for White-British teachers of history to address their inherited 'White privilege' to focus more on the nature of history i.e. the study of history as a discipline, rather than it being used in schools via curriculum for the inculcation of Eurocentric and White-British propagandas. The dominant orientation with British history for trainee-teachers of White-British mono-ethnic background and socialisation speaks to the cultural reproduction of 'Whiteness' in the primary school classroom. Where this connects with the aims and contents of the Key Stage 2 primary school history curriculum, it means that the biggest challenge to decolonising the curriculum is in attempting to reframe a Eurocentric mindset held by the majority of White-British teachers; the default position from which they begin to think about teaching the story of Britain's past.

References

Adi, H. (Ed.). (2019). *Black British History: New Perspectives*. London: Zed Books.
Bhabha, H. (2004). *The Location of Culture*. London: Routledge.
Bhopal, K. (2018). *White Privilege: The Myth of a Post Racial Society*. Bristol: Polity Press.
Boronski, T., & Hassan, N. (2015). *Sociology of Education*. London: Sage.
Bourdieu, P. (1984). *Distinction: A Social Critique of the Judgement of Taste*. London: Routledge.
Bourdieu, P. (1993). *The Field of Cultural Production*. New York: Columbia University Press.
Burns, A. D. (2014). The Jewel in the Curriculum: Teaching the History of the British Empire. *International Journal of Historical Learning, Teaching and Research, 12*(2), 109–121. https://www.ingentaconnect.com/contentone/ioep/herj/2014/00000012/00000002/art00009.
Cameron, D. (2011). *State Multiculturalism has Failed*. Speech at the 47th Munich Security Conference, Munich: Hotel Bayerischer Hof. Retrieved February 6, 2011, from http://www.bbc.co.uk/news/yuk-politics-12371994
Delgado, R., & Stefanic, J. (2012). *Critical Race Theory: An Introduction* (2nd ed.). New York: New York University Press.
Department for Education (DfE). (2013, July). 'History Programmes of Study: Key Stages 1 and 2'. National Curriculum in England. In *The National Curriculum in Britain Framework Document*. London: DfE.
Department for Education (DfE). (2014). *Promoting Fundamental British Values as Part of SMSC in Schools: Departmental Advice for Maintained Schools*. London: Department for Education.
Department for Education (DfE). (2020). *Ethnicity Facts and Figures: School Teacher Workforce*. Retrieved March 4, 2020, from https://www.ethnicity-facts-figures.service.gov.uk/workforce-and-business/workforce-diversity/school-teacher-workforce/latest
Di Angelo, R. (2011). White Fragility. *International Journal of Critical Pedagogy, 3*(3), 54–70. https://libjournal.uncg.edu/ijcp/article/viewFile/249/116.
Domínguez, M. (2019). Decolonial Innovation in Teacher Development: Praxis Beyond the Colonial Zero-Point. *Journal of Education for Teaching, 45*(1), 47–62. https://doi.org/10.1080/02607476.2019.1550605.
Foucault, M. (1980). In C. Gordon (Ed.), *Power/Knowledge* (p. 90). New York: Pantheon.
Frankenburg, R. (1993). *White Women, Race Matters: The Social Construction of Whiteness*. New York: Taylor Francis.
Gaventa, J., Pettit, J., & Cornish, L. (2016). *Bourdieu and 'Socialisation'*. Brighton: Institute of Development Studies, University of Sussex. Retrieved

October 30, 2016, from http://www.powercube.net/other-forms-of-power/bourdieu-and-socialisation/

Gillborn, D. (2008). *Racism and Education: Coincidence or Conspiracy?* London: Routledge.

Gramsci, A. (1971). *Selections from Prison Notebooks.* London: Lawrence and Wishart.

Gramsci, A. (2012). *Selections from Cultural Writings.* London: Lawrence & Wishart Limited.

Harke, H. (1998). Archaeologists and Migration: A Problem of Attitude. *Current Archaeology, 39,* 19–45. https://doi.org/10.1086/204697.

Harke, H. (2011). Anglo Saxon Immigration and Ethnogenesis. *Medieval Archaeology,* 55, 1–28. https://doi.org/10.1179/174581711X13103897378311.

Harnett, P. (2000). History in the Primary School: Re-shaping Our Pasts. The Influence of Primary School Teachers' Knowledge and Understanding of History on Curriculum Planning and Implementation. *International Journal of Historical Learning, Teaching and Research, 1*(1), 5–13. https://www.ingentaconnect.com/content/ioep/herj/2000/00000001/00000001/art00002.

Harris, R. (2013). The Place of Diversity Within History and The Challenge of Policy and Curriculum. *Oxford Review of Education, 39*(3), 400–419. https://doi.org/10.1080/03054985.2013.810551.

Harris, R. (2020). Decolonising the History Curriculum. In M. L. Moncrieffe, R. Race, & R. Harris (Eds.), *Decolonising the Curriculum – Transnational Perspectives, Research Intelligence Issue 142, Spring 2020* (p. 16). London: British Educational Research Association. https://www.bera.ac.uk/publication/spring-2020.

Hobsbawm, E. J. (1959). *Primitive Rebels: Studies in Archaic Forms of Social Movement in the 19th and 20th Centuries.* London: WW Norton.

Hough, A. (2010, October 29). Revealed: David Cameron's Favourite Childhood Book is 'Our Island Story'. *The Daily Telegraph.* Retrieved August 6, 2014, from http://www.telegraph.co.uk/culture/books/booknews/8094333/Revealed-David-Camerons-favourite-lhood-book-is-Our-Island-Story.html

Ladson-Billings, G. (1998). Just What is Critical Race Theory and What's It Doing in a Nice Field Like Education? *Qualitative Studies in Education, 11*(1), 7–24. https://doi.org/10.1080/095183998236863.

Lander, V. (2014). Initial Teacher Education: The Practice of Whiteness. In R. Race & V. Lander (Eds.), *Advancing Race and Ethnicity in Education.* Basingstoke: Palgrave Macmillan.

Marshall, H. E. (1905/2005). *Our Island Story.* Galore Park/Civitas: Tenterden and London.

McCrum, E. (2010). *Teaching History in Postmodern Times: History Teachers' Thinking About The Nature and Purposes of their Subject.* Unpublished EdD Thesis, University of Sussex.

McIntyre, A. (1997). *Making Meaning of Whiteness: Exploring Racial Identity with White Teachers.* New York: State University of New York Press.

Miles, D. (2005). *The Tribes of Britain: Who Are We? And Where Do We Come From?* London: Weidenfield & Nicolson.

Mohanty, C. T. (1994). On Race and Voice: Challenges for Liberal Education in the 1990s. In H. A. Giroux & P. McLaren (Eds.), *Between Borders: Pedagogy and the Politics of Cultural Studies.* New York: Routledge.

Moncrieffe, M., & Moncrieffe, A. (2019). An Examination of Imagery Used to Represent Fundamental British Values and British Identity on Primary School Display Boards. *London Review of Education, 17*(1), 52–69. https://doi.org/10.18546/LRE.17.1.05.

Olusoga, D. (2016). *Black and British: A forgotten history.* London: Pan Macmillan.

Runnymede Trust. (2012). *Making Histories: Developing Young Community Historians.* Runnymede Trust on-line resource. Retrieved August 26, 2014, from http://www.makinghistories.org.uk/

Salili, F., & Hoosain, R. (2001). Multicultural Education: History, Issues and Practices. In F. Salili & R. Hoosain (Eds.), *Multicultural Education: Issues, Policies and Practices* (pp. 1–14). Information Age: Greenwich.

Smart, D. (2010). Going to the Pictures: Learning to See the Life Stories of Minorities Within Majority Narratives. In A.-M. Bathmaker & P. Harnett (Eds.), *Exploring Learning Identity and Power through Life History and Narrative Research* (pp. 97–111). London: Routledge.

Smith, M. K. 2000. Curriculum Theory and Practice. *Encyclopaedia of Informal Education.* Retrieved November 23, 2015, from http://www.infed.org/biblio/b-curric.htm

Sossick, M. (2010). What Impact Does Background Have on Initial Teacher Trainees' Conceptions of Teaching History to Primary School Pupils? *International Journal of the Humanities, 9*(5), 211–221. https://www.researchgate.net/profile/Arzu_Sener/publication/307759795_Women's_Views_on_Old_Age/links/5dbbec3792851c81801dde2f/Womens-Views-on-Old-Age.pdf#page=225.

The Institute For The Study Of Civil Society (CIVITAS). (2015). *'Our Island Story' Free Copies for UK Schools.* Retrieved October 29, 2015, from http://www.civitas.org.uk/islandstory/free.htm

Weekes-Bernard, D. (2013). *Romans Revealed: Who were the Real Romans? A Runnymede Teaching Resource.* London: Runnymede.

Williams, R. (1976). *Keywords.* London: Fontana.

Winder, R. (2013). *Bloody Foreigners: The Story of Immigration to Britain.* London: Abacus.

CHAPTER 4

Orienting with Historical Consciousness

Abstract Historical consciousness can offer a theoretical understanding of how the history curriculum 'Purpose of Study' and the Key Stage 2 primary school aims and contents are positioned with telling the story of Britain's past. This chapter introduces four typologies of historical consciousness: Traditional, Exemplary; Critical; Genetic. In exploring possibilities for decolonising the Key Stage 2 primary school history curriculum, the 'critical' and 'genetic' orientations with 'historical consciousness' are applied to the concept of 'transformative critical multicultural education'. Finally, these typologies of 'historical consciousness' are used to understand how White-British trainee-teachers are orientated with seeing British history, and what they view as most important to them for teaching and learning the story of Britain's past in the Key Stage 2 classroom.

Keywords Historical consciousness • Traditional • Exemplary • Critical • Genetic • Critical multicultural education

Historical Consciousness

Historical consciousness provides a range of theoretical lenses for seeing how human beings position themselves in time and take account of their past (Lee 2004). It seeks to provide a full awareness of the historicity of everything present and the relativity of all opinions through complementary stories; competing stories; and stories that clash with the single dominant

© The Author(s) 2020
M. L. Moncrieffe, *Decolonising the History Curriculum*,
https://doi.org/10.1007/978-3-030-57945-6_4

version of the past (Seixas 2004). The scope of historical consciousness includes individual and collective understandings of the past and the cognitive and cultural factors that shape those understandings (Seixas 2004).

Typologies of Historical Consciousness

Rüsen (2004) provides a typology of historical consciousness through four orientations of seeing and knowing the past in the present and for future possibilities: the 'traditional' perspective; the 'exemplary' perspective; the 'critical' perspective and the 'genetic perspective'. Table 4.1 (below) provides further discussion:

These typologies offer lenses for seeing how the Key Stage 2 primary school history curriculum aims and contents (DfE 2013a) written by policymakers, and primary school trainee-teachers of history are orientated with sharing knowledge for teaching and learning about the story of Britain's past. These typologies also offer ways for seeing how Eurocentrism within the Key Stage 2 primary school history curriculum can be decolonised.

Traditional and Exemplary Orientations

A 'Traditional' historical consciousness is an orientation with history linked to 'maintenance of sense of common origin' and 'traditions' that 'define historical identity' and 'identity formation' as a process in which roles are assumed and played out' (Rüsen 2004, p. 73). Alignment between the 'Traditional' and 'Exemplary' orientation is possible. These can work together to sustain dominant cultural reproduction of historical

Table 4.1 Typologies of historical consciousness

The 'Traditional' Type	The 'Exemplary Type'
'making 'the past significant and relevant to present actuality and its future extension as a continuity of obligatory cultural life patterns over time' (Rüsen 2004, p. 71).	sees 'Tradition' moving 'within a rather narrow frame of empirical reference' and 'viewed as a past recollected with a message or lesson for the present, as didactic' (Rüsen 2004, p. 73).
The 'Critical Type'	The 'Genetic Type'
sees history functioning as 'the tool' by which the continuity of the traditional and exemplary is 'ruptured, deconstructed, decoded—so that it loses its power as a source for present-day orientation' (Rüsen 2004, p. 75).	sees that 'change is of the essence and is what gives history its sense' (Rüsen 2004, p. 76).

discourses so that 'historical identity is constituted by one's assuming the regularity of cultural and life patterns' (Rüsen 2004, p. 74). The 'Exemplary' orientation sees 'Tradition' moving 'within a rather narrow frame of empirical reference' and 'viewed as a past recollected with a message or lesson for the present, as didactic' (Rüsen 2004, p. 73). These orientations speak in line with the statutory directive in the Key Stage 2 primary school history curriculum (DfE 2013a, p. 4) for teaching and learning through Eurocentric lives and experiences of settlement on the British Isles by Anglo Saxons and Scots'; through 'Viking and Anglo-Saxon struggle', 'Scots invasions'; and 'Viking raids and invasion'. The experiences of European ethnic groups of the past are positioned as 'traditional' and 'exemplary' sources of knowledge and understanding about 'nation building' and 'national identity' on the British Isles. A default position for acquiring knowledge and understanding is given by these particular Eurocentric experiences from the past, centred as the source of cultural universals to maintain a cultural identity for British people in the present and future (Seixas 2004).

950 Missing Years of Mass-Migration and Settlement

When looking closely at the Key Stage 2 primary school history curriculum aims and contents for teaching British history, there are no teaching and learning directives or guidance for knowledge and understanding to be developed on histories and lives of Black-British people. In fact, there is no attention at all given to migrant people of non-European heritage. When the national curriculum chronology for Key Stage 2 primary school history stops at the year 1066, Key Stage 2 teachers have no further statutory directives or explicit guidance to teach pupils about the next 950 years of mass-migration and settlement to the British Isles for knowing about the continuance of 'nation building' and the development of 'national identity' through cultural diversity. The national curriculum 'Purpose of Study' states that it 'will help pupils gain a coherent knowledge and understanding of Britain's past' and it 'helps pupils to understand the complexity of people's lives, the process of change, the diversity of societies and relationships between different groups, as well as their own identity' (DfE 2013a, p. 1). How are the processes of change; diversities in society; and a sense of own identity (especially for pupils born in Britain of non-European parentage) supposed to be learnt when 950 years of British history to the current date concerning mass-migration and settlement to the British Isles is missing from the curriculum?

It may be suggested that the Key Stage 3 history curriculum (DfE 2013b) can offer teaching and learning coverage. For example, through the unit: 'a study of an aspect of social history, such as the impact through time of the migration of people to, from and within the British Isles' (DfE 2013b, p. 5). However, as pointed out in Chap. 2, this unit of study is 'non-statutory guidance'. This means that secondary schools and teachers of history are neither obliged to, nor held to account on whether they teach this to their students or not. Regardless of this, why should pupils have to wait until they enter Key Stage 3 education to potentially gain some knowledge on the broader histories of mass-migration and settlement to the British Isles, and British multicultural diversity beyond that of Eurocentrism?

Seeing the Past in the Present

There are a plethora of stories unwritten by the Key Stage 2 primary history curriculum concerning mass-migration, settlement, and cross-cultural 'encounters' between people on the British Isles over the ages. One recent example is of the British citizens from the twentieth century African-Caribbean 'Windrush Generation' (see Fryer 2010; Phillips and Phillips 1998; Sewell 1998), their involvement in uprisings across cities in England related to their violent "struggles" with the oppressive and racist White-British led political system (Moncrieffe 2017, 2018, 2019, 2020; Adi 2019; Fryer 2010; Sewell 1998; Gilroy 1992/1987). These violent "struggles" between migrant minority-ethnic people and the settled majority-ethnic people resulted in a need to develop new ways of living in peaceful co-existence on a culturally diverse British Isles. For example, as a result of these cross-cultural encounters, a number of Race-Relations Acts have been written into law since the 1960s. Today, the Equality Act (2010) emerges from these. This speaks to building a nation that respects the ethnic, cultural and gender differences of all British citizens.

I see that the more recent cross-cultural encounters and the resulting need to develop new approaches to understanding and living in peaceful co-existence on a culturally diverse British Isles, can be examined alongside the violent cross-cultural encounters that occurred between the 'Viking (minority migrant people) and Anglo-Saxon (majority settled people) struggles' (DfE 2013a). Pupils in Key Stage 2 primary school are already being taught by their teachers to learn about these violent 'struggles', and how these came by 'invasions', migration and settlement. The outcome of these 'struggles' were treaties (Downham 2008; Gordon 1937) for 'nation building' and peaceful co-existence on a culturally diverse British Isles.

Critical and Genetic Orientations

In Chap. 1, I stated that decolonising the curriculum involves the creative dissemination of alternative ways in seeing the past as relevant to knowing about present times, and the future. This can provide many possibilities in teaching and for pupils' advanced learning, through acquiring new currencies of knowledge. This way offers a more equitable means of transaction in teaching, learning and education for all. I see decolonial thinking for teaching and learning as challenging the imposed epistemes (Foucault 1980) in education, and this is where Rüsen's (2004, p. 75) 'critical' orientation as reflecting 'elements of a counter-narrative to the one behind the stone-engraving' (the traditional and exemplary types) must become central to praxis. Rüsen writes 'the easiest way to do this is to state that the story is untrue' (Rüsen 2004, p. 74). It is not that the story of 'Viking and Anglo-Saxon struggles' and the nation building that emerged from this is 'untrue'. It is more that this not the only story that can be learnt from when thinking about 'nation building' and 'national identity'. The national curriculum 'Purpose of Study' states it 'will help pupils … to understand … the diversity of societies and relationships between different groups, as well as their own identity' (DfE 2013a, p. 1). What I suggest is, as opposed to the directed approach to teaching and learning the story of Britain's migrant past through 'Anglo-Saxon and Viking Struggles' (DfE 2013a, p. 4), the use and application of experiences and stories from more recent times on the British Isles can add alternative narratives to this teaching and learning. In doing so, pupils would be able to relate more recent history to stories of the distant past.

A 'critical' orientation with historical consciousness for seeing the story of Britain's migrant past can challenge and transform the Eurocentric aims and contents of the Key Stage 2 primary school curriculum. Using this lens for teaching and learning about the history of cross-cultural encounters between people of the British Isles can advance the view of how the past relates strongly to our current conditions: How do pupils see themselves in that history? What can they learn about themselves and their parents? What can they learn about other individuals and their ethnic identities? What are the future possibilities for a culturally diverse society? To what extent could teaching and learning about the history of cross-cultural encounters support teaching and learning about the stated fundamental British values of 'mutual respect' and 'tolerance' (DfE 2014) between British people? I see that this relates to the 'genetic' orientation with historical consciousness: That 'change is of the essence, and is what gives history its sense' (Rüsen 2004, p. 76). This sees the ongoing legacy of the past, but at the same time, it comprehends radically changed present circumstances and mores (Seixas 2004).

History as Transformative Critical Multicultural Education

Decolonising the Key Stage 2 primary school history curriculum can occur by adopting the lenses of 'critical' and 'genetic' historical consciousness in orientation with the concept of 'transformative' critical multicultural education (May and Sleeter 2010; Banks 1997, 2009; McLaren 2002). Banks (2009) writes:

> The transformative (of critical multicultural education) changes the basic assumptions of the existing curriculum, and *aims to help students understand concepts and issues from different ethnic and cultural perspectives* … to become aware that knowledge is not culture-free but rather constructed through the perspectives of those who have power. *In the transformative approach, students learn the dominant narratives but also alternative narratives.* In the end it is hoped that students will be able to think critically about whose narratives are used and the consequences of this. Changing the basic assumptions of the existing curriculum.

'Transformative' critical multicultural education means centring teaching and learning through alternative narratives of marginalised minority-ethnic groups in a society. Through transformative critical multicultural education, the dominant 'traditional' and 'exemplary' orientations of knowing and seeing the story of Britain's past in the present, and future possibilities is challenged by 'critical' and 'genetic' orientations for ways of seeing and knowing (Rüsen 2004).

Trainee-Teacher Orientations

How were the White-British trainee-teachers of primary school history that I introduced in Chap. 2 orientated in their thinking about the story Britain past through Rüsen's (2004) four typologies of historical consciousness? I asked them: **What does the story of 'British history' mean to you?** Beginning with trainee-teachers of majority mono-ethnic White-British backgrounds and socialisation.

Dawn:	To me 'British History' means significant events which took place in Britain. It is to me, the series of events which built Britain to what it is today. I associate British history to the Normans, The Middle Ages, The Tudors, Civil War and Revolution, Empire, The Slave Trade, Victorians World War One, World War Two and then the transition and focus of modern Britain. To me, it's about how Britain's nations have shaped the Empire.
Victoria:	About how we built our British Empire through Saxons, Romans, Vikings. Also, it means learning about historical figures that have shaped British history.
James:	To me, this term means history such as Monarchy, significant events such as World War Two.
Tom:	The development, creation and changes of the British Empire and its impact on the modern day.

The thoughts shared by Dawn, Tom, Victoria and James about the story of British history see them orientating with statements in the aims and contents of the Key Stage 2 and Key Stage 3 history curriculum. The collective thinking from Dawn, Tom, Victoria and James is on the 'British Empire' and British 'Monarchy'. This indicates their orientations with British history through Rüsen's (2004) 'Traditional Type' of historical consciousness, where 'historical identity is constituted by one's assuming the regularity of cultural and life patterns' (Rüsen 2004, p. 74). Victoria's words: 'how we built our British Empire' points to her sense of ownership and White-British pride. This can be related to a YouGov poll from 2014 which found that among the British public, most think the British Empire is something of which to proud (59%) rather than ashamed (19%) (Dahlgreen 2014). Victoria's thinking about mass-migration and settlement speaks to a Eurocentrism: 'Saxons, Vikings, Romans'. This thinking replicates the contents of Key Stage 2 primary history curriculum.

The White-British trainee-teachers of multi-ethnic backgrounds and socialisation generally indicated a broader sense of cultural and ethnic diversity according to their thinking about the story of British history.

Emma:	British history to me means all of the significant events which took place from the past and the present in order to form the way we are today. For example, the mix of cultures over the years has widened foods etc. available to us.

Rachel: British history encompasses the origin of the islands, the movement of people and range of people that have inhabited Britain. How they have helped to shape what our country—and countries—are today. The story of Britain, the story of people, the stories of each child that we teach including personal histories of the children we teach: Where are their families from? How has this shaped them as a person? What significant events have happened in their lifetime. The story of Britain, the story of people, the stories of each child that we teach.

Both Emma's and Rachel's orientations with historical consciousness point towards Rüsen's 'genetic' type where they are seeing that 'change is of the essence' (Rüsen 2004, p. 76) e.g. 'events which took place from the past and the present' and what this may suggest about the future. This can be linked with Emma's and Rachel's sense of a developing 'culture' and 'nationhood' in the British Isles over the ages. Emma discusses British history as a 'mix of cultures over the years'—a multicultural perspective in articulating what she sees as the making of a culturally diverse Britain and British identity. Rachel also appears to place her emphasis with seeing British history from a specific view of diversity in groups of people in Britain over the ages i.e. the 'range of people that have inhabited Britain over the ages'.

Summary

The national curriculum 'Purpose of Study' states that it 'will help pupils gain a coherent knowledge and understanding of Britain's past' and 'helps pupils to understand the complexity of people's lives, the process of change, the diversity of societies and relationships between different groups, as well as their own identity' (DfE 2013a, p. 1). However, the aims and contents for Key Stage 2 primary school history teaching and learning about mass-migration and settlement to the British Isles is Eurocentric. A 'traditional' orientation with historical consciousness is the only perspective of British history given by the Key Stage 2 primary history school curriculum. It is a Eurocentric orientation that can influence the reproduction of dominant cultural discourses in the teaching and learning about the story of Britain's migrant past through narrow frames of empirical reference (Rüsen 2004). This is evidenced by 'traditional' and 'exemplary' Eurocentric orientations with historical consciousness articulated by trainee-teachers of majority mono-ethnic White-British backgrounds and socialisation. They generally see British history through the lives of European minority-ethnic groups of the past e.g. Anglo-Saxons; Vikings; Normans; and, stories of the British Monarchy. This perspective aligns with statements for teaching and learning about British history in the aims and contents of the Key Stage 2 and Key Stage 3 history curriculum. Trainee-teachers of multi-ethnic backgrounds and socialisation orientate with British history in relation to a story of culturally diversity in people developing over the ages. These trainee-teachers of multi-ethnic backgrounds and socialisation appear to apply 'critical' and 'genetic' perspectives of historical consciousness for seeing the possibility of teaching and learning through 'transformative' critical multicultural education (May and Sleeter 2010; Banks 1997, 2009; McLaren 2002).

References

Adi, H. (Ed.). (2019). *Black British History: New Perspectives*. London: Zed Books.
Banks, J. A. (1997). *Educating Citizens in a Multicultural Society. Multicultural Education Series*. New York: Teachers College Press.
Banks, J. A. (Ed.). (2009). *The Routledge International Companion to Multicultural Education*. Abingdon: Routledge.
Dahlgreen, W. (2014). *The British Empire is 'Something to be Proud of'*. Retrieved January 4, 2018, from https://yougov.co.uk/topics/politics/articles-reports/2014/07/26/britain-proud-its-empire
Department for Education (DfE). (2013a, July). 'History Programmes of Study: Key Stages 1 and 2'. National Curriculum in England. In *The National Curriculum in Britain Framework Document*. London: DfE.
Department for Education (DfE). (2013b, July). 'History Programmes of Study: Key Stages 3 and 4'. National Curriculum in England. In *The National Curriculum in Britain Framework Document*. London: DfE.
Department for Education (DfE). (2014). *Promoting Fundamental British Values as Part of SMSC in Schools: Departmental Advice for Maintained Schools*. London: Department for Education.
Downham, C. (2008). Vikings in England. In *The Viking World* (pp. 365–373). London: Routledge. https://pdfs.semanticscholar.org/f359/8a1e7ddca405602a7792ba0e0c0d68e13848.pdf#page=366.
Foucault, M. (1980). In C. Gordon (Ed.), *Power/Knowledge* (p. 90). New York: Pantheon.
Fryer, P. (2010). *Staying Power*. London: Pluto Press.
Gilroy, P. (1992/1987). *There Ain't No Black in the Union Jack*. London: Routledge.
Gordon, E. V. (1937). The Date of Æthelred's Treaty with the Vikings: Olaf Tryggvason and the Battle of Maldon. *The Modern Language Review*, 32(1), 24–32.

HMSO. (2010). *The Equality Act 2010*. Retrieved September 20, 2016, from http://www.legislation.gov.uk/ukpga/2010/15/pdfs/ukpga_20100015_en.pdf

Lee, P. (2004). Understanding History. In P. Seixas (Ed.), *Theorizing Historical Consciousness* (pp. 129–164). Toronto: University of Toronto Press.

May, S., & Sleeter, C. E. (Eds.), (2010). *Critical Multiculturalism: Theory and Praxis*. London: Routledge.

McLaren, P. (2002). White Terror and Oppositional Agency: Towards a Critical Multiculturalism. In *Critical Pedagogy and Predatory Culture* (pp. 131–158). London: Routledge.

Moncrieffe, M. L. (2017). Teaching and Learning About Cross-Cultural Encounters Over the Ages Through the Story of Britain's Migrant Past. In R. Race (Ed.), *Advancing Multicultural Dialogues in Education* (pp. 195–214). Cham: Palgrave Macmillan. https://doi.org/10.1007/978-3-319-60558-6_12.

Moncrieffe, M. L. (2018). *Arresting 'Epistemic Violence': Decolonising the National Curriculum for History*. London: British Educational Research Association. Retrieved March 4, 2020, from https://www.bera.ac.uk/blog/arresting-epistemic-violence-decolonising-the-national-curriculum-for-history

Moncrieffe, M. L. (2019). An Approach to Decolonising the National Curriculum for Key Stage 2 History in Initial Teacher Education. In M. L. Moncrieffe, Y. Asare, R. Dunford, & H. Youssef (Eds.), *Decolonising the Curriculum – Teaching and Learning about race Equality, Issue 1, July 2019* (p. 12). Brighton: Centre for Learning and Teaching, University of Brighton. https://cris.brighton.ac.uk/ws/portalfiles/portal/6443632/Decolonising_the_curriculum_MONCRIEFFE_32_pages_4th_July.pdf.

Moncrieffe, M. L. (2020). Decolonising Narratives of Mass Migration in the National Curriculum for Key Stage 2 History. In M. L. Moncrieffe, R. Race, & R. Harris (Eds.), *Decolonising the Curriculum – Transnational Perspectives, Research Intelligence Issue 142, Spring 2020* (p. 18). London: British Educational Research Association. https://www.bera.ac.uk/publication/spring-2020.

Phillips, T., & Phillips, M. (1998). *Windrush: The Irresistible Rise of Multi-Racial Britain*. London: Harper Collins.

Rüsen, J. (2004). Historical Consciousness: Narrative Structure, Moral Function, and Ontogenetic Development. In P. Seixas (Ed.), *Theorizing Historical Consciousness* (pp. 63–85). Toronto: University of Toronto Press.

Seixas, P. (2004). Introduction. In P. Seixas (Ed.), *Theorizing Historical Consciousness* (pp. 3–20). Toronto: University of Toronto Press.

Sewell, T. (1998). *Keep on Moving: The Windrush Legacy: the Black Experience In Britain from 1948*. London: Voice Communications Group Limited.

CHAPTER 5

Centring the Black Experience in Key Stage 2 Primary School British History

Abstract This chapter presents memories from the author and his mother on their interpretations of the cross-cultural encounters between their migrant African-Caribbean minority-ethnic group people and White-Britain in Brixton, London in 1981. This recent historical experience is juxtaposed with similarities from the distant past, and analysed to consider the potential it may hold for advancing teaching and learning about British history in the Key Stage 2 primary school classroom.

Keywords 'Purpose of study' • African-Caribbean • Black-British • Memories • Diasporic imagination

PERSONAL HISTORY

I am first generation Black-British born of African-Caribbean immigrant parents. My mother and father came to England as children from Jamaica in the early 1960s. My parents followed my Jamaican grandparents and my Jamaican great-grandmother. All had migrated to England in the early 1950s as part of the 'Windrush Generation' (Fryer 2010; Phillips and Phillips 1998; Sewell 1998). My grandparents lived in England for some years before deciding to migrate to the United States of America, and then returning to Jamaica in the 1980s. My maternal grandmother remained in England, in Brixton, south London. I visited her regularly as a child, with my mother and my siblings.

© The Author(s) 2020
M. L. Moncrieffe, *Decolonising the History Curriculum*,
https://doi.org/10.1007/978-3-030-57945-6_5

This thinking about my family's relatively short existence and being on the British Isles; and their lives and experiences as a minority-ethnic people amongst a majority White-British ethnic people, shaped my interest to explore new ways of teaching and learning about mass-migration and settlement on the British Isles for Key Stage 2 primary school history. I knew that the Key Stage 2 primary school history curriculum (DfE 2013) statutory directives focused on mass-migration and settlement through the 'struggles' between 'Viking (minority migrant people) and Anglo-Saxons (majority settled people)'. As a child, I had witnessed the 'struggles' involving African-Caribbean people and a hostile White-Britain in 1981, in Brixton, London. In my thinking, I saw this as an opportunity to connect the past with present, for generating perceptions of the future, and for advancing possibilities in teaching and learning through the Key Stage 2 primary school history curriculum.

The 'Purpose of Study'

I perceived that there could be much value in using and applying my own memories of the Brixton 1981 'struggles', for considering how it could advance the potential of teaching and learning about the story of Britain's migrant past with trainee-teachers of Key Stage 2 primary school history. This is because the national curriculum 'Purpose of Study' (DfE 2013, p. 1) states that teachers:

> will help pupils gain a coherent knowledge and understanding of Britain's past' for helping 'pupils to understand the complexity of people's lives, the process of change, the diversity of societies and relationships between different groups, as well as their own identity.

This is difficult to achieve. The Key Stage 2 primary school history curriculum chronology of British history stops at the year 1066. Whilst Eurocentric lives and histories are provided either as statutory directives, or as guidance for teaching and learning, the lives and histories of non-White groups of people (non-European) who have also migrated and settled on the British Isles remain absent from the Key Stage 2 primary school history curriculum aims and contents.

A statutory unit for teaching and learning is given, for pupils to 'study of an aspect or theme in British history that extends pupils' chronological knowledge beyond 1066' (DfE 2013, p. 5). With this there is over 950 years since 1066 to the current day that could generate a wide amount of possibilities for the Key Stage 2 primary school history teacher to explore with children cultural diversity including Black-British histories and experiences. However, what has been learnt from Chaps. 3 and 4 is that the majority of White trainee-teachers of primary school history are led by Eurocentric and White-British histories in their thinking and what my become their choices for themes for study. Eurocentric and White-British starting points are also the guidance given by the Key Stage 2 primary school history curriculum for unit of study that extends pupils' chronological knowledge beyond 1066 (DfE 2013, p. 5):

- the changing power of monarchs using case studies such as John, Anne and Victoria
- changes in an aspect of social history, such as crime and punishment from the Anglo-Saxons to the present or leisure and entertainment in the twentieth Century
- the legacy of Greek or Roman culture (art, architecture, or literature) on later periods in British history, including the present day
- a significant turning point in British history, for example, the first railways or the Battle of Britain

There is no apparent pathway beyond Eurocentrism for pupils to gain knowledge of ethnically diverse people of the British Isles in the past, and how this relates to the present and future.

I saw that a generation of knowledge from the history of my minority-ethnic group people; their lives and experiences of mass-migration to the British Isles, would be personally empowering. I saw that this could also provide an approach to teaching and learning that met clearly with national curriculum 'Purpose of Study' statements on helping 'pupils gain a coherent knowledge and understanding of Britain's past', and helping 'pupils to understand the process of change, the diversity of societies and relationships between different groups, as well as their own identity.' (DfE 2013, p. 1).

Involving My Mother

I shared with my mother the desire I had to tell the stories of our migrant minority-ethnic group's experiences. I explained that I wanted to make a record of these for future presentation with trainee-teachers of primary school history; for gaining understanding on their thinking and potential ideas for teaching and learning, using Black-British history as the starting point to a story of Britain's past. I was confident that my mother's lived experiences as a child immigrant of African-Caribbean migration and settlement to the British Isles in the twentieth century, and her experiences of Brixton 1981 would provide rich insights. She agreed to share her memories with me through a conversation. I informed her that I would share the transcripts of our conversation with trainee-teachers of primary school history, and in doing so, I would also protect our identities. This is because I wanted to present our stories to the trainee-teachers of primary school history as being of no particular African-Caribbean immigrant parent and their Black-British born child's reflections. My mother agreed to this process.

In our writing about African-Caribbean mass-migration and settlement; Brixton 1981 and the Black-British experience, my mother and I produced short personal written accounts of our memories. I acknowledge that the use of memory in seeking to advance knowledge and learning does not come without criticism.

Critiquing Memory

Delamont (2007, p. 2) suggests that use of researcher/author memory as a prime source of the data generation is an approach to social research that is 'literally lazy and also intellectually lazy.' This is because experiential accounts of evidence deriving from the self and memory have the potential for producing heavily biased data. This raises caution on the reliability of the stories given through those memories; the credibility and validity in production of the data (Ellis et al. 2011; Delamont 2007). The argument here is that memory is fallible, in that it is impossible to recall or to report events in language that exactly represents how those events were lived and felt (Ellis et al. 2011). Chang (2008, p. 5) agrees, but takes a less radical view in suggesting that memory as data bank for social research can be 'both a friend and foe'. On one hand, the power of memory can offer a huge and rich amount of data given through remembered moments that are considered to have significantly impacted the trajectory of a person's life (Ellis 2007). On the other hand, the potential pitfall in using memory is where it selects, shapes, limits and distorts in recollection of episodes from the past (Chang 2008). However, Van Manen (1990, p. 54) argues that new knowledge generated from 'one's own experiences are also the possible experiences of others' to be shared. This is supported by Hayler (2011, p. 16) who asserts that 'power of memory comes not from precision or accuracy, but from how we relate to our constructions and re-constructions of the past as we are now' to help with future responses. With these competing perspectives of memory, it is useful to return to Chap. 1 where I stated: decolonising the curriculum involves the creative dissemination of alternative ways for seeing the past in the present, for future possibilities in the teaching and pupils' learning. This way can offer new currencies of knowledge, used as a more equitable means of transaction in teaching, learning and education for all. This is what I see emerging from my mother's and my own accounts of our migrant, minority-ethnic group, African-Caribbean and Black-British experiences, through our memories of Brixton 1981. These are accounts that cannot stand alone as objective truths of the event they describe. They are open to scrutiny and interpretation. However, I see the value drawn from the accounts through my meaning making, and in understanding our memories for learning new ways of knowing from critical contextual analysis.

Mother's Memories: Brixton 1981

The African-Caribbean people were getting fed up with the police stopping and searching a lot of African-Caribbean people, so the riot started. That day I was worried about my family who are African-Caribbean, so I took a 37 bus with four children. It was only going to Clapham Common as Brixton was a no-go area. So, I walked around the side roads to get there. On arrival, Brixton looked like World War Three. A lot of shops and buildings were burnt out, all except one African-Caribbean pub. There were lots of police cars, and fire engines were still outing the fires. When I did get to my mother's house, the riot did not get that far. I had to walk back to Clapham Common to go home.

Images of Brixton 1981 (Moncrieffe 2018)

'SWAMP 81'

It has been well documented that the African-Caribbean community in Britain including their Black-British children through their increased presence in White-British society faced racist discrimination when seeking to gain homes and jobs (Adi 2019; Gilroy 1987/1992; Sewell 1998; Phillips and Phillips 1998). Brixton 1981 is argued as their response to the persistent abuse that they faced from racist White-British led gangs such as the Metropolitan Police Force. Operation Swamp 1981 was the institutional harassment (Gilroy 1987/1992; Phillips and Phillips 1998) of African-Caribbean people and their Black-British children by the Metropolitan Police. This was fuelled by hostile language about immigration in Britain from Conservative Party Leader Margaret Thatcher (1978) who suggested that White-Britain was 'being swamped' by 'other' darker skinned ethnic and cultural groups. The experiences of African-Caribbean people 'getting fed up with the police stopping and searching' remembered by my mother was 'revenge swamping' (Gilroy 1987/1992; Scarman 1981) by the institutional powers of White-Britain through the Metropolitan Police Force.

INVASION OR INVITATION?

From a Key Stage 2 primary school history teaching and learning perspective, the phrase 'being swamped' could be used to consider 'the struggles' between 'Viking and Anglo-Saxons' and 'invasion' and 'settlement' (DfE 2013, p. 4). Majority settled people of the British Isles (Anglo-Saxons) 'being swamped' by 'invaders' such as minority migrant people (Vikings) in the eighth century could be related to twentieth century African-Caribbean and White-British 'struggles' (Moncrieffe 2017, 2018, 2019, 2020). However, it should be remembered that a major difference between the minority group Viking people and the minority group African-Caribbean people is that the latter were not 'invaders' to the British Isles. In fact, they were invited by the British Government to settle in Britain after World War Two as citizens; to support with rebuilding the British economy, developing a new post-war society and with that a new national identity (Phillips and Phillips 1998; Sewell 1998; Winder 2013). A derogatory discourse towards 'invading' African-Caribbean people has been infiltrated by White supremacists such as Enoch Powell (1968/2007) to plant fear into the minds of the White-British public. Thatcher's (1978) language about 'being swamped' added to Powell's derogatory and poisonous discourse.

My Memories: Brixton 1981

We were walking in the aftermath of what I had seen on television the previous day. We walked pass cars that had been burnt out, smashed glass on the floor; large cylinder iron dustbins burnt out and left in the road. We walked past shops that had windows either smashed out or boarded up. The streets were emptier of cars and vehicles that usually rushed by on Brixton Road by the red bricked town hall building. As we crossed the highway of Brixton Road and headed towards Coldharbour Lane, I looked to the left to see the police cars and police vans parked in the distance towards Stockwell. Vans and cars were smashed out. The place was something like in the aftermath of a cyclone. We continued through Coldharbour Lane. We approached the market—The Grandville Arcade and it was dead. For me, it always was a low feeling when I saw it closed, but that day was worse. That place was the heart of Brixton: busy and bubbling with life. Now, it was lifeless. We walked past more rubbish and debris on the floor. Something had disturbed Brixton, and it was what I saw on the television—the fighting between the Police and Black people. We continued towards Loughborough Park to my Nan's house.

Contested Notions of Brixton 1981

The British Broadcasting Corporation (BBC), applied the word 'riot' as a negative discourse and portrayal of Brixton 1981 (BBC 2011). However, Fryer (2010, p. 395) writes:

> 'Riot', being a four-letter word, is excellent for headlines; but its use to describe what were in fact uprisings by entire inner-city populations, Black and White together, served to obscure the true nature and causes of the events.

The reference to an 'uprising by entire inner-city populations'; and 'Black and White together' by Fryer (2010) implies that Brixton 1981 was not just a revolt against inequities linked to racial tensions, but because of wider forms of social inequality under the policies of Thatcher's Conservative government of the time. Gilroy (1987/1992) describes Brixton 1981 as the African-Caribbean community in their 'struggle' for equality and social justice. Ouseley (2016) understands Brixton 1981 as 'disturbances' in the 'struggle for race equality'. Scarman (1981, p. 73) reported on Brixton 1981 as social 'disorders'. Interpretations of Brixton 1981 are contested. This relates somewhat to the uncertainty of what happened in my recounts: 'something like in the aftermath of a cyclone' and 'something had disturbed Brixton.'

From Morant Bay 1965 to Brixton 1981

Lea (2005, p. 1) suggests that riots are 'theatres in which grievances of the poor and socially excluded have been played out'. Taking the action to rise up against a system on the part of people without any other means of representing their interests, aiming to defend themselves from abuse, attack and harassment of various types, in the quest for freedom, has a long history (Hobsbawn 1959). There is a history of African-Caribbean people leading their uprisings (riots) with an ultimate aim to resist and emancipate themselves from White oppression. For example, the 1816 slave revolt in Barbados; the 1831 slave revolt in Jamaica known as 'The Baptist War'; and the 1865 slave revolt in Morant Bay, Jamaica (Greenwood and Hamber 1980). These uprisings of the nineteenth century led by African-Caribbean people are repeated by their children in their cross-cultural encounters with White-British people on the British Isles in the twentieth century in Brixton 1981. As Phillips and Phillips (1998, p. 353) write:

> The Caribbean migrants brought with them a determined Black nationalism and anti-colonialism all over the globe in the person of Marcus Garvey. The same Caribbeans carried with them folk memories and descriptions of legendary rebellions, from the Maroons and Paul Bogle in Jamaica to the series of slave martyrs all over the Caribbean who bore African names—Quashie (Akwesi), Quackoo (Akweku), Cuffee (Akofi), all leaders of slave rebellions in the Caribbean.

In understanding the sense of determination for justice and freedom described above, it is perhaps not surprising then that African-Caribbean people as migrants and immigrants invited to live and work in White Britain by the government, when faced with a continued reality of oppression, racism and poverty that their ancestors fought so hard to defeat, responded to this through Brixton 1981.

Balancing Voices

Goodley (1998, p. 123) discusses how management and control of the voice in presentation of stories can become a shifting 'locus of power' between the research and the researched. I saw that the conversation that I would have with my mother about our memories was not for me to reshape her world view. I aimed to prompt and challenge her perspectives and responses in my facilitation of the dialogue. This was for seeing how the past relates to our present and the future, and for keeping a sense of focus and structure in our conversation. My mother had the power, control, and freedom to decide how she wanted to respond to my prompts and challenges. My role was to provide a perspective as her Black-British born child, now viewing the past and present as an adult.

Conversation Between Me and My Mother

Me: What does Brixton mean to you?
Mother: When I first came off the plane from Jamaica at 10 years old that's where I lived for 24 years and loved it for its multicultural life.
Me: What do you mean by 'multicultural'? Do you think people were living well together in harmony and respect for each other?
Mother: Living there as a young woman, looking back from my point of view, yes.
Me: When you used to take us to Brixton to visit Nan, it always used to feel like a trip away from our home on the council estate to another culture of London: different people; crowds. I always felt the presence of a wide variety of people in Brixton: the Jamaican baker's shop where we bought patties and bread and the familiar distinctive smell of baking; the loud voices of the market traders—mainly White people selling fish; the reggae music either inside or outside the market. I think now and then of Brixton as a settlement for Black people. Mainly Jamaican people. What do you think?
Mother: No. Most of the Black people I knew wanted to earn their money and go back home to Jamaica. But unfortunately, many didn't.

Me: Looking back now, what I mean by a settlement is a place where migrant people establish a base for their community. Do you think Brixton is down as the seminal settlement base for Jamaican people? A bit like the Normans arriving in Hastings?

Mother: I don't think so. Before they sent for their children, my father came first to get money, then my mother and my grandmother.

Me: So would you say Brixton was more of temporary settlement than a permanent settlement?

Mother: Yes. Well alright. Once they had earned some money they could go back.

Me: Was it almost like a temporary settlement for your father?

Mother: Yes, and for my grandmother and her husband. Eventually, they went back.

Me: But what about their grandchildren?

Mother: It's up to the grandchildren. We came over here when we were children. When we grew up as adults and had our children we were allowed to decide where we wanted to stay.

Me: Although you were adults. Did you think that you could actually go back to Jamaica?

Mother: No.

Me: Why not?

Mother: Because I spent most of my life over here. I am a citizen. That's for me.

Me: What about the riots in Brixton? Would you describe them as riots or something else?

Mother: Black people were standing up for themselves and they said, "Enough is enough!" They were standing up against racism. The Police didn't believe that something like that could have happened. No Police were on guard. There was no shield. The Police were defenseless. The Police were stopping and searching Black people. Black people couldn't get work. They didn't want to be on benefits. Everytime the Police see Black people, they think they are thieves.

Me: When I was a child during the time of it. I didn't know the reasons as to why there was rioting. But what I do know now as I have understood things is that rioting, tension… I am going to relate this to more contemporary issues. Like for example the most recent riot in London a few years ago, when

	Mark Duggan (Black man) got shot by the Police.[1] Is this simply a continuance of what happened 30 years ago, you know… Police harassment of Black people or do you think things may have improved and developed? Because what I see now in my mind is almost like a chronology of events involving a struggle for Black people that started even before Brixton. The Notting Hill riots of the fifties; more riots in the eighties and recently. Do you think Black people and their history, and their struggles have served to improve their standing in Britain in any way? You know… Has the government done anything to help them? Because there is a clear chronology of struggle.
Mother:	I don't think so. But I think they try to do things undercover. There is still undercover racism.
Me:	Do you think that the history of Black people in Britain over the last 50 or 60 years could be presented in a chronological way through these events and used for teaching in schools?
Mother:	In Brixton, you have Windrush Square[2], local museums, Bob Marley. But this should have been done long before riots. The Black community fought for these things. That should have been done a long time ago.
Me:	So how significant do you think the riots are not just in Brixton but all over Britain in which Black people were involved? Are these part of British history?
Mother:	We don't count in British history.
Me:	But these events have happened in Britain and there has been some reaction from the government via policies, such as Race Relations Acts. Even when you think other incidents such the murder of Stephen Lawrence… interesting that didn't cause a riot, but it did create some reaction through the Macpherson inquiry and report didn't it?

---

[1] Mark Duggan, a 29-year-old Black-British man was shot and killed by the Metropolitan Police in Tottenham, North London on 4th August 2011. Duggan's death resulted in public protests in Tottenham which escalated into riots across London and other English cities.

[2] Windrush Square is an open public space in the centre of Brixton in South London. It recognises the important contribution of the African Caribbean community to the area. It was the HMT Empire Windrush that in 1948 brought to the United Kingdom from Jamaica the first large group of post-war West Indian migrants (almost 500), who on arrival were temporarily housed less than a mile away from Coldharbour Lane in Brixton.

Mother: Sometimes Race Relations Acts work for people and sometimes it doesn't. Do they teach Black history in school?
Me: Is this Black history?
Mother: Yes.
Me: Is this British history?
Mother: A bit of both.
Me: It happened in Britain, so I think it must be British history. What benefit would children all over Britain have by learning about the history riots like this in Britain?
Mother: Windrush Square. If you are going to call it Windrush Square they should say that this stands for Black people who came over here. And don't forget it was their children and grandchildren who rioted.
Me: And stood up for their rights? Do you think people rioting in Brixton felt displaced? Feeling alien in Britain.
Mother: Depends on how they were brought up. Depends if they have been back to Jamaica. The council poured lots of grants in after the riots. But Brixton wasn't for Black people. But now, Brixton is on the map.
Me: What is it on the map for?
Mother: The riots. Yes. Because that was one of the biggest riots.
Me: So, what kind of legacy does Brixton leave?
Mother: Nothing for us.
Me: Yes. But … the legacy of the riots and why there were riots. For people, do you think the word 'Brixton' means riots?
Mother: Ha! Yes. When I was younger Brixton was full of Black people. Now when you go down there, it is not the same.
Me: Would you say that particular era or moment of time is something that should be remembered through teaching about history?
Mother: It's gone. Dead.
Me: How should be it remembered?
Mother: Between the 1950s and 1980s there was a large population of Black people. Now it seems like it has gone.
Me: You mentioned Windrush Square. Do you think they should be taught about Windrush as well as the riots? Do you think children should learn about this in school?
Mother: Depends how they take it. What do you think?

Me: Well, I think it was social struggle in Britain similar to civil rights movement in the USA during the 1960s based on fighting against oppression, discrimination and was calling for an immediate change.

Mother: "Get up! Stand up!" Standing up for their rights and this can be traced back. So yes. It could be taught in schools. Do you think many children will want to hear about violence and riots?

Me: Well… in primary schools, children learn about the Viking invasions. They were a minority-ethnic group of the past who caused violence and bloodshed in their attacks. Whilst Black people in Brixton, you could argue that were standing up for themselves.

HISTORY AND BIOGRAPHY WITHIN SOCIETY

The conversation between my mother and me is an example of what Chang (2008, p. 6) has described as 'interactive introspection'. We consider, reflect and discuss to see how our minority-ethnic group identities have been situated socially and culturally through our experiences of mass-migration and settlement and through our interactions with White-Britain. We apply the sociological imagination (Wright-Mills 1959) as a reflective approach to our discussion, learning about the relations between history and biography within society. My mother and I see the African-Caribbean and Black-British 'struggles' from the past in White-Britain as continuing in current times. An example of this is where my mother says: 'Black people were standing up for themselves and they said: "Enough is enough!" They were standing up against racism. Everytime the Police see Black people, they think they are thieves.' These are her thoughts on the discrimination and oppression faced by 'Black people' in Brixton in 1981. It is a 'struggle' with White-Britain she perceives as entrenched: 'I think they try to do things undercover. There is still undercover racism.' I also consider the sense of 'struggle' through 'a chronology of cross-cultural encounters involving Black-British people and 'the most recent riot in London a few years ago, when Mark Duggan (Black man) got shot by the Police.' I ask: 'Is this simply a continuance of what happened 30 years ago?' The recent 'Windrush Scandal' (see for example: Bulman 2020; Agerholm 2018; Gentleman 2018) provides clear evidence of the continued 'struggle' for African-Caribbean and Black-British people in

White-Britain. Child immigrants to the British Isles who came from Jamaica after the end of World War Two, having lived and worked in Britain as citizens for most of their lives have as adults recently faced the ignominy of deportation. This 'institutional ignorance and thoughtlessness' came from an egregious policy of racial discrimination led by successive Conservative governments through Prime Ministers Theresa May and her successor Boris Johnson (Williams 2018).

Diasporic Imagination

My mother and I speak as one, but we do so through different lenses of a diasporic imagination (Vertovec 1996). We articulate our views of the past and present, through motives and meaning-making influenced by our conscious and sub-conscious levels of acculturation and socialisation with White-Britain. I see my mother's perspective reflecting the marginalisation felt by African-Caribbean and Black British-people when she says: 'We don't count in British history.' I cannot disagree with her feeling this way through the experiences of racial discrimination she and I have both experienced. Still, I am positioned with thinking that we (African-Caribbean and Black-British people) do count for something quite significant and valuable through our stories of mass-migration and settlement to the British Isles, and as part of British history. I aimed to facilitate the conversation as neutrally as I could, but I found myself influencing the discussion from a view of the value in our history, pulling my mother along with me with questions and prompts. For example where I say: 'But these events have happened in Britain'; 'It happened in Britain, so I think it must be British history and 'it was social struggle in Britain ... based on fighting against oppression, discrimination'. My mother is inspired and responds with: "Get up! Stand up!' words of resistance given by Black Jamaican musicians Bob Marley and Peter Tosh, both significant Black cultural icons during the 1970s and early 1980s speaking up to empower African-Caribbean people in their diaspora from Africa, and their daily encounters with the oppressive nature of Eurocentrism. Still, when I put to my mother: 'what kind of legacy does Brixton leave', and perhaps expecting a positive response from her, she countered with: 'Nothing for us... It's gone. Dead.' I see that her words refer to the death of a larger vibrant African-Caribbean community in Brixton; one that has now been colonised by White-British middle-class gentrification; Whitewashing the African-Caribbean past (Whettle 2015). To some extent, this justifies my mother's view: 'Brixton wasn't for Black people'. But, African-Caribbean and Black-British people were the ones that put Brixton 'on the map'.

The 'Struggle' for Race Equality

Cross-cultural 'struggles' of the 1980s were not confined to Brixton, London, but were widespread across Britain where African-Caribbean communities had settled. Most notably in St. Paul's, Bristol; Handsworth, Birmingham; Toxteth in Liverpool; Hyson Green, Nottingham; and Moss Side, Manchester (Winder 2013). The 1980s represent a significant period of British history that could be used for teaching and learning about cross-cultural encounters in the story of Britain's past. Particularly, where the national curriculum for history 'Purpose of Study' states that teachers 'will help pupils gain a coherent knowledge and understanding of Britain's past' for seeing 'the process of change, the diversity of societies and relationships between different groups, as well as their own identity (DfE 2013, p. 1). However, the Key Stage 2 history curriculum aims and contents provides no explicit directive or guidance to teach for learning about 'the diversity of societies' in Britain on which learning through mass-migration and settlement, and cross-cultural encounters appear to be central. I see that Brixton 1981 should be viewed as one of many opportunities to learn from the past, for teaching and learning about race equality in the present, and in the future. Primary school teachers' use and application of this episode from British history would offer them a starting point for teaching and learning about cross-cultural 'encounters', and society's approach to 'nation building' through a culturally diverse people seeking to live together in co-existence.

'Black-British History is Starved of Oxygen'

It may be argued that Key Stage 2 primary school history teachers could develop pupils' learning about Brixton 1981 through the statutory directive: 'study of an aspect or theme in British history that extends pupils' chronological knowledge beyond 1066', and through guidance to select 'a significant turning point in British history' (DfE 2013, p. 5). I can see the opportunity and value in using Brixton 1981 through this guidance, as a Black-British man, teacher, and as a critical curriculum thinker. However, what about White-British primary school teachers? Would they see the same opportunities and value as I do? Chapters 3 and 4 has shown that the majority of White trainee-teachers of that sample group—future qualified teachers—reproduce Eurocentric and White-British histories in their thinking and choices for themes for study, aligned to the Key Stage 2 primary school history curriculum.

The Key Stage 2 primary school history curriculum offers no explicit opportunities for teaching and learning which centres Black-British history and Black-British experience. Black-British history is starved of oxygen by the suffocation of 'Whiteness' (Eddo-Lodge 2017). It is concerning that Black-British primary school teachers must deliver a national history curriculum that consists of statutory aims and contents focused totally on White-British history. For me, as a Black-British man, teacher and educator, this omission of the Black-British experience from the Key Stage 2 primary history curriculum is an offence.

My accounts of Britain's past centre attention on the experiences of migrant African-Caribbean people; their Black-British children and their struggles with White-Britain in Brixton 1981. This is an example of how the Key Stage 2 primary school history curriculum must be decolonised for advancing inclusive teaching and learning. Brixton 1981 represents a recent and significant episode of British history concerning cross-cultural 'struggles' between migrant minority people and settled majority people. From a Key Stage 2 primary school history curriculum teaching and learning perspective, this invites the opportunity for teachers an pupils to apply historical consciousness (Rüsen 2004; Seixas 2004) for exploring the potential of patterns in past experiences on the British Isles, such as through mass-migration and settlement, and 'struggles' between 'Viking (minority migrant people) and Anglo-Saxons (majority settled people).

REFERENCES

Adi, H. (Ed.). (2019). *Black British History: New Perspectives*. London: Zed Books.

Agerholm, H. (2018). *Windrush: Government Admits 83 British Citizens May Have Been wrongfully Deported Due to Scandal But Will Only Apologise to 18*. Retrieved November 29, 2019, from https://www.independent.co.uk/news/uk/home-news/windrush-government-deportations-british-citizens-uk-caribbean-home-office-rudd-javid-a8501076.html

British Broadcasting Corporation (BBC). (2011). *Brixton Riots: Archive*. Retrieved August 4, 2016, from http://www.bbc.co.uk/news/uk-13012055

Bulman, M. (2020). *Home Office Showed 'Institutional Ignorance and Thoughtlessness' Towards Race, Windrush Report Finds*. Retrieved March 23,

2020, from https://www.independent.co.uk/news/uk/home-news/windrush-report-scandal-generation-news-racism-latest-a9411186.html

Chang, H. (2008). *Autoethnography as Method*. Walnut Creek: Left Coast Press.

Delamont, S. (2007). Arguments Against Auto-Ethnography. In *Qualitative Researcher: Issue 4, February 2007* (pp. 2–4). Cardiff: ESRC National Centre for Research Methods, Cardiff University. http://www.leeds.ac.uk/educol/documents/168227.htm.

Department for Education (DfE). (2013, July). 'History Programmes of Study: Key Stages 1 and 2'. National Curriculum in England, In *The National Curriculum in Britain Framework Document*, July 2013, London: DfE.

Eddo-Lodge, R. (2017). *Why I'm No Longer Talking to White People About Race*. London: Bloomsbury Circus.

Ellis, C. (2007). Telling Secrets, Revealing Lives: Relational Ethics in Research with Intimate Others. *Qualitative Enquiry, 13*(1), 3–9. https://doi.org/10.1177/1077800406294947.

Ellis, C., Adams, T., & Bochner, A. P. (2011). Autoethnography: An Overview. *Qualitative Social Research, 12*(1), 1–13. https://doi.org/10.2307/23032294.

Fryer, P. (2010). *Staying Power*. London: Pluto Press.

Gentleman, A. (2018). *'My Life is in Ruins': Wrongly Deported Windrush People Facing Fresh Indignity*. Retrieved November 20, 2019, from https://www.theguardian.com/uk-news/2018/sep/10/windrush-people-wrongly-deported-jamaica-criminal-offence

Gilroy, P. (1987/1992). *There Ain't No Black in the Union Jack*. London: Routledge.

Goodley, D. (1998). Stories About Writing Stories: Reappraising the Notion of the 'Special' Informant with Learning Difficulties in Life Story Research. In P. Clough & L. Barton (Eds.), *Articulating with Difficulty: Research Voices Inclusive Education*. London: Sage.

Greenwood, R., & Hamber, S. (1980). *Emancipation to Emigration*. London and Basingstoke: Macmillan Education.

Hayler, M. (2011). *Autoethnography, Self-Narrative and Teacher Education*. Rotterdam/Boston/Taipei: Sense Publishers.

Hobsbawn, E. J. (1959). *Primitive Rebels: Studies in Archaic Forms of Social Movement in the 19th and 20th Centuries*. London: WW Norton.

Lea, J. (2005). From Brixton to Bradford: Ideology and Discourse on Race and Urban Violence in the United Kingdom. *The Howard Journal of Criminal Justice, 44*(2), May 2005. https://www.cambridge.org/core/journals/canadian-journal-of-law-and-society-la-revue-canadienne-droit-et-societe/article/security-sovereignty-and-nonstate-governance-from-below/621025B3F3DD09EB3053E4E864907E59

Moncrieffe, M. L. (2017). Teaching and Learning About Cross-Cultural Encounters Over the Ages Through the Story of Britain's Migrant Past. In R. Race (Ed.), *Advancing Multicultural Dialogues in Education* (pp. 195–214). Cham: Palgrave Macmillan. https://doi.org/10.1007/978-3-319-60558-6_12.

Moncrieffe, M. L. (2018). *Arresting 'Epistemic Violence': Decolonising the National Curriculum for History*. London: British Educational Research Association. Retrieved March 4, 2020, from https://www.bera.ac.uk/blog/arresting-epistemic-violence-decolonising-the-national-curriculum-for-history

Moncrieffe, M. L. (2019). An Approach to Decolonising the National Curriculum for Key Stage 2 History in Initial Teacher Education. In M. L. Moncrieffe, Y. Asare, R. Dunford, & H. Youssef (Eds.), *Decolonising the Curriculum – Teaching and Learning about race Equality, Issue 1, July 2019* (p. 12). Brighton: Centre for Learning and Teaching, University of Brighton. https://cris.brighton.ac.uk/ws/portalfiles/portal/6443632/Decolonising_the_curriculum_MONCRIEFFE_32_pages_4th_July.pdf.

Moncrieffe, M. L. (2020). Decolonising Narratives of Mass Migration in the National Curriculum for Key Stage 2 History. In M. L. Moncrieffe, R. Race, & R. Harris (Eds.), *Decolonising the Curriculum – Transnational Perspectives, Research Intelligence Issue 142, Spring 2020* (p. 18). London: British Educational Research Association. https://www.bera.ac.uk/publication/spring-2020.

Ouseley, H. (2016). *The Struggle for Race Equality*. Retrieved August 4, 2016, from http://www.runnymedetrust.org/histories/index.php?mact=OralHistories,cntnt01,default,0&cntnt01qid=35&cntnt01returnid=20

Phillips, T., & Phillips, M. (1998). *Windrush: The Irresistible Rise of Multi-Racial Britain*. London: Harper Collins.

Powell, E. (1968). *Rivers of Blood* (Reprinted in *The Daily Telegraph*, November 6, 2007). Retrieved October 31, 2016, from http://www.telegraph.co.uk/comment/3643823/Enoch-Powells-Rivers-of-Blood-speech.html

Rüsen, J. (2004). Historical Consciousness: Narrative Structure, Moral Function, and Ontogenetic Development. In P. Seixas (Ed.), *Theorizing Historical Consciousness* (pp. 63–85). Toronto: University of Toronto Press.

Scarman, L. G. (1981). *The Scarman Report: The Brixton Disorders 10–12 April 1981*. London: Penguin Books.

Seixas, P. (2004). Introduction. In P. Seixas (Ed.), *Theorizing Historical Consciousness* (pp. 3–20). Toronto: University of Toronto Press.

Sewell, T. (1998). *Keep on Moving: The Windrush Legacy: the Black Experience in Britain from 1948*. London: Voice Communications Group Limited.

Thatcher, M. (1978). *TV Interview for Granada World in Action ("Rather Swamped")*. Retrieved November 13, 2015, from http://www.margaretthatcher.org/document/103485

Van Manen, M. (1990). Investigating Experience as We Live It. In *Researching Lived Experience: Human Science for an Action Sensitive Pedagogy* (pp. 53–76). New York: SUNY.

Vertovec, S. (1996). Diaspora. In A. Ellis-Cashmore (Ed.), *Dictionary of Race and Ethnic Relations* (4th ed., pp. 89–101). London: Routledge.

Whettle, A. (2015). *The Gentrification of Brixton: How Did the Area's Character Change So Utterly?* Retrieved September 3, 2016, from http://www.independent.co.uk/news/uk/home-news/the-gentrification-of-brixton-how-did-the-areas-character-change-so-utterly-a6749276.html

Williams, W. (2018). *Windrush Lesson Learned Review by Wendy Williams.* Retrieved March 23, 2020, from https://www.gov.uk/government/publications/windrush-lessons-learned-review

Winder, R. (2013). *Bloody Foreigners: The Story of Immigration to Britain.* London: Abacus.

Wright-Mills, C. (1959). *The Sociological Imagination.* Harmondsworth: Penguin.

CHAPTER 6

Transforming White-British Trainee-Teachers' Thinking Through Black-British History

Abstract In this chapter, White-British trainee-teachers of primary school history provide their responses on how they would use the stories from migrant African-Caribbean people and Black-British people for teaching and pupils learning through the 'Purpose of Study', aims and contents of the Key Stage 2 primary school history curriculum. The trainee-teachers discuss mass-migration, settlement, and cross-cultural encounters on the British Isles in recent times and the distant past. They discuss possibilities for advancing teaching and learning in primary school history and for teaching and learning about fundamental British values. The trainee-teachers are able to generate ideas from an orientation with 'critical' historical consciousness, enabling them to see praxis through transformative' critical multicultural education.

Keywords Fundamental British values • 'Transformative' critical multicultural education • Praxis

Teaching and Learning Through Cross-Cultural Encounters

How can teaching and learning become more of a 'cross-cultural encounter'? I ask this question with a view that teaching students to reflect about different cultures will allow a space for cultural understandings to increase (Race 2015). I stated in Chap. 3 the biggest challenge to decolonising the

© The Author(s) 2020
M. L. Moncrieffe, *Decolonising the History Curriculum*,
https://doi.org/10.1007/978-3-030-57945-6_6

primary school history curriculum through teaching and learning may be in attempting to reframe Eurocentric mindsets; the default position from which trainee-teachers of White-British mono-ethnic background and socialisation begin to think about teaching the story of Britain's past. I was therefore interested in testing my question with White-British trainee-teachers of primary school history, aiming to understand their interpretations of twentieth century cross-cultural encounters in Brixton, London, in 1981 involving African-Caribbean (migrant minority-ethnic group) people of the 'Windrush Generation' (Fryer 2010; Phillips and Phillips 1998; Sewell 1998) and their Black-British children in 'struggles' with White-Britain (settled majority-ethnic people). I wanted to know how White-British trainee-teachers of primary school history would use the Black-British perspective as their starting point for historical enquiry around mass-migration and settlement on the British Isles over the ages.

Trainee-Teachers

Diana, Anne and Catherine were three White-British trainee-teachers of primary school history that I recruited as my volunteers to take part in a Focus-Group discussion. They emerged from the 21 trainee-teachers of primary school history (see Chap. 2) that had responded to my questionnaire and my interviews on teaching and learning about mass-migration and settlement to the British Isles through the Key Stage 2 primary school history curriculum. Diana, Anne, and Catherine had reproduced Eurocentric and White-British ideas in their thinking about British history through their responses to the questionnaire and interviews. Table 6.1 gives a view of their background identities:

Sharing the Black-British Experience

I shared with Diana, Anne and Catherine each a fully transcribed version of the written reflections and conversation produced by my mother and me (see Chap. 5) concerning our memories of childhood; of mass-migration and settlement to the British Isles; and, the cross-cultural encounters with White-Britain, in Brixton, London, in 1981. I presented the transcripts to them as accounts given by no particular African-Caribbean immigrant parent and their Black-British born child. I provided Diana, Anne and Catherine 2 weeks each to read the transcripts of the written reflections and conversations, alongside printed copies of the

Table 6.1 Identities of trainee-teachers focus-group discussion

Name	Ethnic group	Age group	Neighbourhood as a child and teenager	Ethnic make-up of Primary school	Ethnic make-up of Secondary School	Experience and study of history as a subject
Diana	White-British	18–25	Generally mono-ethnic White-British	Generally mono-ethnic White-British	Generally mono-ethnic White-British	GCSE
Anne	White-British/Irish	18–25	Generally mono-ethnic White-British	Generally mono-ethnic White-British	Generally mono-ethnic White-British	A level
Catherine	White-British	18–25	Generally mono-ethnic White-British	Generally mono-ethnic White-British	Generally mono-ethnic White-British	GCSE AS level A level

'Purpose of Study', aims and contents of the Key Stage 2 primary school history curriculum. These artefacts were brought to the Focus Group discussion to stimulate our conversation.

'THE CHANCE TO CONTRAST'

Diana and Catherine linked their thoughts about the transcripts with the Key Stage 2 primary school history curriculum directive (DfE 2013, p. 5) 'a study of an aspect or theme in British history that extends pupil's chronological knowledge beyond 1066':

Diana: I suppose it links to a study of an aspect or a theme in British history that extends pupils' chronological knowledge beyond 1066 on page 5. And I think it has links to, just reading this here on page four, the 'Viking and Anglo-Saxon struggle…'
Catherine: Yeah [in agreement with Diana].
Diana: …the Viking raids and invasions. They are quite …and then Anglo-Saxon laws and justice and invasions, death and resistance and all of those sorts of words might be associated

	with... with riots and change and stuff like that and so you have got this chance to contrast.
Catherine:	It's all migration I suppose isn't it?
Diana:	Yeah [in agreement with Catherine].
Catherine:	Well. Like the settlement of Anglo-Saxons. You can… Like, when they [parent and child] are talking about… Brixton being the ethnic minority… settlement. They settled there. And you could almost say like [to children]: 'Where did Anglo-Saxons settle…?'
Diana:	"Settle" [spoken in synchrony with Catherine].
Catherine:	….and you can kind of make relations that way.

Diana and Catherine sense congruency with the past and more recent times concerning the story of Britain's migrant past associated with 'resistance'; 'riots'; 'change' and 'settlement'. They see this for teaching and learning as 'a chance to contrast'; to develop historical enquiry further i.e. 'Like when they (parent and child) are talking about… Brixton being the ethnic minority… settlement. They settled there. And you could almost say like: Where did Anglo-Saxons settle…?' This shows that the twentieth century cross-cultural encounters in 1981 in Brixton, London being theorised for use as a 'study of an aspect or a theme in British history that extends pupils' chronological knowledge beyond 1066' (DfE 2013, p. 5) for teaching and learning about British history when planted in the minds of White-British trainee-teachers of primary school history.

VISUALISING PRAXIS

Further use of the written reflections produced by my mother and me that informed Diana's, Catherine's and Anne's ideas for future approaches to teaching and learning came from a sense of their visualising praxis through historical enquiry:

Catherine:	It says like: "We were walking in what was the aftermath of what I'd seen on television." That paragraph. When I read this, I wrote next to it: "How would you [children] feel if this were your home?" You could read out the writing and get children to imagine like well: How would I feel walking through this? Like, this is where I lived and grew up.

Diana: Yes. I think that's what is really powerful, and there should be a place for using reflections or narratives and getting children to interview people first-hand.
Anne: Drama as well.

Diana's comments on the potential use of conversation between my mother and me can be associated with connecting personal and local histories (Runnymede Trust 2012) for demonstrating ways that migration as a concept and historical process has impacted on the lives and experiences of all individuals living in modern Britain.

Catherine added further comments on potential use of the conversation between my mother and me for approaches to practice in relation to future historical enquiry concerning what constitutes as British history:

Catherine: Yeah. The first thing that came to my mind for me at the end of it, was where they [parent and child] were talking about: "Well is it British history then?" and the parent says: "I think Black people in Britain and in London are tarred with the same brush" and things like that. You could... like the parent isn't convinced that it's British history. So, I think that could be quite an interesting thing for children to... almost investigate like: "Is it British history?" They could investigate that themselves and kind of decide for themselves.

COMPARISONS OF THE MIGRANT EXPERIENCE

Diana and Catherine identify Eurocentrism as a narrow direction for teaching and learning about mass-migration and settlement in the national curriculum for history chronology and in the Key Stage 2 primary school history curriculum aims and contents (DfE 2013):

Diana: There is nothing post 1066 about explicit migration. Pre that, it discusses movement through the Stone Ages; the Iron Ages; the Roman empire ...
Catherine: Yes. [in agreement with Diana].
Diana: ... Anglo-Saxons. But post that, unless... unless you take it on yourself as teacher, you are not going to get that.

Diana, Anne and Catherine all agree that the conversation between my mother and me could be applied alongside the Key Stage 2 primary school history curriculum for examining comparisons of migrant experiences over the ages i.e. Saxon migration and settlement in juxtaposition with Afro-Caribbean migration and settlement:

Catherine: I think it is important like… the parent says, "My father came first to get money." So, looking at why they moved. Like the comparison between… like if… a Jamaican-Black immigrant parent moved for money, then what did the Saxons move for?
Anne and Diana: Yeah [in synchrony and in agreement with Catherine].
Catherine: Compare it. Is there any change or movement over time? They [Saxons] moved for resources which is kind of like money. So, you can make comparisons on like: "Has it really changed that much?" What similarities there still are and what differences there are as well.

This discussion led by Catherine seeks to explore a route to what may be a 'common ground' of human experience learnt via British history, 'where Black and White can meet' (Samuel 2003) through their shared stories of migration and settlement.

'FUNDAMENTAL BRITISH VALUES'

In their discussion of the conversation between my mother and me, Diana, Catherine and Anne also saw this as an opportunity for shaping approaches to teaching and learning about 'fundamental British values' (DfE 2014):

Catherine: Where the child says, "stood up for their rights", that's a kind of freedom of speech.
Anne: Yeah, that's 'Britishness'. Because it's about being able to do that; being able to express what you want and protest without having any backlash from the government which I don't know is always 100% true. But, that to me is what is all about living in a country where you should be allowed to say what you want.
Catherine: So maybe… equality. Yeah maybe the equality side of it. Like: "Why just us?" Like: "Why not that person as well?"

Anne: Yes. You could say that is a protest because you're being discriminated against and you're protesting against it.
Catherine: Yeah [in agreement with Anne].
Diana: I think like if we are going to be talking about 'tolerance' and 'equality', if we are going to be teaching those British values, then we are going to need to have multicultural perspectives within the curriculum.

Diana's comment is a call to policymakers to include multicultural perspectives as part of the aims and contents of the Key Stage 2 primary school history curriculum so as to advance the teaching and learning of 'fundamental British values' (DfE 2014). This relates to what Harris (2013) discusses as an opportunity to reframe the national curriculum for history, in recognition of a modern diverse make-up in British society from a broader multi-ethnic and eclectic perspective.

Reflection

Diana, Anne, and Catherine are young, White and female trainee-teachers of primary school history. I am an experienced Black-British male academic, and former primary school teacher. It may be argued that the power dynamic between us; our contrasting ethnic identities; and our motives for engagement in the Focus Group discussion could possibly have led them to produce responses that they perceived would satisfy what they may have thought I wanted to hear. However, throughout the process, Diana, Anne and Catherine were generally interested in thinking about and exploring new possibilities to curriculum interpretation. The very fact that they had given their time to take part in the questionnaire and interviews (Chap. 2) and had volunteered again to participate in this Focus Group discussion indicates their enthusiasm and commitment. Their confident engagement with one another during the Focus Group discussion included many shared endorsements and developments of each other's point of view. This indicated their sense of being uninhibited by my presence during the process of the Focus Group conversation.

Diana, Anne and Catherine made strong links between the transcribed conversation of my mother and me, and teaching and learning about the story of Britain's past through mass-migration and settlement in connection with the 'Purpose of Study', aims and contents of the Key Stage 2 primary school history curriculum. They used experiences from migrant African-Caribbean and Black-British people for advancing their thinking on teaching and learning about 'fundamental British values' (DfE 2014). They spoke together from the perspective of 'critical' historical consciousness (Rüsen 2004) shifting what counts as knowledge away from the dominant vantage point of Eurocentrism (Sleeter 2010) associated with the Key Stage 2 primary school history curriculum. Their focus on British history through the lives and experiences of marginalised minority-ethnic groups in society demonstrated Banks' (2009) notion of 'transformative' critical multicultural education.

References

Banks, J. A. (Ed.). (2009). *The Routledge International Companion to Multicultural Education*. Abingdon: Routledge.
Department for Education (DfE). (2013, July). 'History Programmes of Study: Key Stages 1 and 2'. National Curriculum in England. In *The National Curriculum in Britain Framework Document*. London: Department for Education.
Department for Education (DfE). (2014). *Promoting Fundamental British Values as Part of SMSC in Schools: Departmental Advice for Maintained Schools*. London: Department for Education.
Fryer, P. (2010). *Staying Power*. London: Pluto Press.
Harris, R. (2013). The Place of Diversity Within History and the Challenge of Policy and Curriculum. *Oxford Review of Education, 39*(3), 400–419. https://doi.org/10.1080/03054985.2013.810551.
Phillips, T., & Phillips, M. (1998). *Windrush: The Irresistible Rise of Multi-Racial Britain*. London: Harper Collins.
Race, R. (2015). *Multiculturalism and Education* (2nd ed.). London: Bloomsbury.
Runnymede Trust. (2012). *Making Histories: Developing Young Community Historians*. Runnymede Trust On-line Resource. Retrieved August 25, 2014, from http://www.makinghistories.org.uk/
Rüsen, J. (2004). Historical Consciousness: Narrative Structure, Moral Function, and Ontogenetic Development. In P. Seixas (Ed.), *Theorizing Historical Consciousness* (pp. 63–85). Toronto: University of Toronto Press.
Samuel, R. (2003). A Case for National History. *International Journal of Historical Teaching, Learning and Research, 3*(1), 69–73. https://www.ingentaconnect.com/contentone/ioep/herj/2003/00000003/00000001/art00010.
Sewell, T. (1998). *Keep on Moving: The Windrush Legacy: The Black Experience in Britain from 1948*. London: Voice Communications Group Limited.
Sleeter, C. (2010). Decolonizing Curriculum. *Curriculum Inquiry, 40*(2), 193–203. https://doi.org/10.1111/j.1467-873X.2010.00477.x?journalCode=rcui20.

CHAPTER 7

Opportunity, Action and Commitment

Abstract This chapter reflects on possibilities for teaching and learning about Britain's migrant past through the story of cross-cultural encounters in Brixton, London, in 1981 involving African-Caribbean minority-ethnic group people of the 'Windrush Generation', and their Black-British children in 'struggles' with White-Britain. This is discussed with existing professional studies and resources that provide opportunities for teaching and learning in the primary school about mass-migration and settlement to Britain over the ages through the lives and experiences of non-White peoples. 'Critical curriculum thinking' is advocated for advancing practice, and for seeing the value in connecting British history, 'race' and 'cultural diversity' for teaching and learning.

Keywords Critical curriculum thinking • Black-British history • Fundamental british values

BUILDING ON THEORY AND KNOWLEDGE

Chapters 5 and 6 explored the possibilities for teaching and learning a story of Britain's migrant past through cross-cultural encounters, in Brixton, London, in 1981 involving migrant African-Caribbean minority-ethnic group people of the 'Windrush Generation', and their Black-British children in 'struggles' with White-Britain. My approach to advancing Key Stage 2 primary school history teaching and learning on notions of mass-migration and settlement for decolonising the curriculum builds upon existing professional studies and resources. For example, Hann (2004) brought attention to primary school teachers and pupils the possibility of using stories of mass movements of people to Britain, through slavery to indentured labour, Partition and the two World Wars. This connects notions of the migrant and immigrant experience of past and present together as a form of historical enquiry. Sheldrake and Banham (2007, p. 39) produced a local history study of the large Caribbean community in Ipswich, Suffolk, seeing this as an ideal opportunity for collecting local and individual stories which form a part of the nation's history—the 'big picture' story of migration to Britain. Hawkey and Prior (2011, p. 244) presented the potential value in classroom study through a 'lens of migration status', stating that this focus can 'enable us to better understand how perspectives are affected by trans-migration backgrounds, experiences and histories.' The Runnymede Trust (2012) devised the resource *Making Histories* for connecting personal and local histories, and for seeking to exemplify how migration as concept and historical process has impacted on the lives and experiences of all individuals living in modern Britain. In discussing this, Alexander et al. (2015, p. 15) write: 'The focus was to bring invisible and marginalised histories to the fore [where] these aspects of British history … have been largely absent from the new curriculum.' In her study of 'How many people does it take to make an Essex man?' McCrory (2013, p. 8) explores 'fresh ways of construing similarity and difference in past lives.' This includes exploring the notion of cross-cultural encounters; and, the changing nature of language between migrant groups from the past who have settled in Britain and how their ethnogenesis (Harke 1998, 2011 has shaped the present local identity.

The professional studies and resources presented above speak to advancing Key Stage 2 primary school history teaching and learning through a clear focus on the cultural histories and the diversity of ethnic groups who have come to settle on the British Isles over the ages. However, adopting this approach in teaching and learning requires a commitment by primary school teachers to become 'critical curriculum thinkers' (Harris 2020).

'CRITICAL CURRICULUM THINKING'

It is argued by Harris (2020) that teachers should be empowered to be able to engage in questions and debate on the 'what' and the 'why' of curriculum implementation in their teaching and learning. Not simply to become 'curriculum makers', but to become 'critical curriculum thinkers' that actively evaluate the educational worth of given curriculum aims and contents. This call for greater professional agency seems reasonable. However, Callender (2019) argues that limited time, if any, is afforded by Initial Teacher Education providers to the professional development of primary school trainee-teachers on themes such as 'race' and 'cultural diversity' for curriculum implementation. This suggests that opportunities are scarce for primary school trainee-teachers to become equipped with the theoretical knowledge and skills so that they can appreciate the value in connecting British history, 'race' and 'cultural diversity' in their teaching and for pupils learning.

Genuine 'action' and 'commitment' (Chilisa 2012) and advancement in decolonial work by Initial Teacher Education providers (Lander 2014) is needed. Ono-George (2019) argues that Initial Teacher Training needs to force its students, especially White-British students in the majority, out of their comfort zones of White privilege, so that their future practice can become engaged, anti-racist and decolonial. Primary school trainee-teachers of mono-ethnic White-British backgrounds and socialisation should be forced to apply a greater sense of reflexivity in their 'critical curriculum thinking'. This means engaging more consciously on the *what* and the *why* of curriculum implementation (Harris 2020).

Why Not Black-British History?

An example of the *what* and the *why* of curriculum implementation can be related to teaching and learning about 'race equality'. The Key Stage 1 history curriculum (pupils aged 5–7) offers an opportunity for pupils to learn about American Civil Rights activist Rosa Parks, and her defiance of racism in White America during the 1950s and 1960s (DfE 2013, p. 2). *Why* have British history curriculum policy writers afforded twentieth century African-American history higher status over any examples of twentieth century Black-British history concerning 'race-equality'? *What* about the Bristol Bus Boycott of 1963 led by Paul Stephenson? This was a Civil Rights protest for 'race equality' in Britain. *Why* has this not been referenced for guidance and use in teaching and learning by the Key Stage 1 history curriculum? Is this because there is fear among White people that accepting Britain's difficult history with race means somehow admitting defeat? (Eddo-Lodge 2017). This 'White-denial' (Chantiluke et al. 2018; Eddo-Lodge 2017) has silenced the potential of curriculum teaching and learning about 'race equality' through the Bristol Bus Boycott in 1963. I see that the Bristol Bus Boycott in 1963 would be a better starting to point than the story of Rosa Parks for British pupils to learn about 'race-equality'. This would also make Black-British history central to deepening teaching and learning for all about the fundamental British values such as 'mutual respect' and 'tolerance' (DfE 2014).

Summary

What can be learnt from the theories and case-studies provided in this book? Trainee-teachers of mono-ethnic White-British backgrounds and socialisation generally perceive British history as rooted to stories concerning the lives of White European minority-ethnic groups of the past e.g. Anglo-Saxons; Normans and the elites of society i.e. the Monarchy. These orientations with 'traditional' and 'exemplary' types of historical consciousness (Rüsen 2004) align with the Eurocentric default position of the Key Stage 2 primary school history curriculum. This perception of what is meant by British history held by trainee-teachers of mono-ethnic White-British backgrounds and socialisation suggests that teaching and learning about British history in their classrooms is likely to be through narrow Eurocentric lenses.

When White-British trainee-teachers provided their responses to using Black-British history as a stimulus for teaching and pupils learning in connection with the national curriculum 'Purpose of Study' and Key Stage 2 primary school history aims and contents, they were able to orientate with a 'critical' historical consciousness (Rüsen 2004) for seeing praxis through 'transformative' critical multicultural education' (Banks 2009). This is an important process of learning that needs to become embedded and assessed in initial teacher education; and, in primary school teaching and learning in order to illustrate the importance and commitment given to anti-racism. A transformation in policy and practice is necessary. The Key Stage 2 primary school history curriculum aims and contents provide no explicit directive or guidance for teaching and learning about the migration to the British Isles of non-White peoples over the ages; those peoples who have contributed to shaping the cultural and racial diversity of societies in Britain today. Therefore, examining for congruency in lived experiences of cultural diversity in the distant past and recent times should be central to teaching and learning British history in the Key Stage 2 primary school classroom. Pupils will be able to relate this to current and future conditions of a continually developing and fluid multicultural British society.

My example of Key Stage 2 primary school history curriculum teaching and learning about the twentieth century cross-cultural encounters, in Brixton, London, in 1981 gives a central voice to Black-British lives and experiences. This approach to decolonising Eurocentrism in the primary school history curriculum can offer primary school teachers and their pupils a route to a broader knowledge and understanding of Britain's migrant past, including an understanding of relationships between different ethnic groups in the present and how these can become more cohesive in the future.

I have stated in this book that the biggest challenge to decolonising the curriculum is in attempting to reframe a Eurocentric mindset held by the majority of White-British teachers; the present default position from which they begin to think about teaching the story of Britain's past. White-British primary school trainee-teachers of mono-ethnic White-British backgrounds and socialisation need to see and understand how their inherited 'White privilege' narrows their perspectives and approaches to teaching and learning history. Their centring of Black-British narratives of history as an equal if not better alternative to the White-British norms through orientations with 'critical' and 'genetic' types of historical consciousness (Rüsen 2004) will help to challenge and transform the way in which they currently think about British history. Advancing 'critical curriculum thinking' in this way can foster epistemic innovation in white-British primary school teachers for decolonising Eurocentrism in the Key Stage 2 primary school history curriculum.

REFERENCES

Alexander, C., Weekes-Bernard, D., & Chatterji, J. (2015). *History Lessons: Teaching Diversity in and Through the History National Curriculum.* London: Runnymede.

Banks, J. A. (Ed.). (2009). *The Routledge International Companion to Multicultural Education.* Abingdon: Routledge.

Callender, C. (2019). Race and Race Equality: Whiteness in Initial Teacher Education. In P. Miller & C. Callender (Eds.), *Race, Education and Educational Leadership in England: An Integrated Analysis* (pp. 15–36). London: Bloomsbury.

Chantiluke, R., Kwomba, B., & Athinangamso, N. (2018). *Rhodes Must Fall: The Struggle to Decolonise The Racist Heart of Empire.* London: Zed Books.

Chilisa, B. (2012). *Indigenous Research Methodologies.* Los Angeles: Sage Productions.

Department for Education (DfE). (2013, July). 'History Programmes of Study: Key Stages 1 and 2'. National Curriculum in England. In *The National Curriculum in Britain Framework Document*. London: DfE.

Department for Education (DfE). (2014). *Promoting Fundamental British Values as Part of SMSC in Schools: Departmental Advice for Maintained Schools*. London: Department for Education.

Eddo-Lodge, R. (2017). *Why I'm No Longer Talking to White People About Race*. London: Bloomsbury Circus.

Hann, K. (2004). Migration: The Search for a Better Life? *Primary History, Summer 2004*, 31–37.

Harke, H. (1998). Archaeologists and Migration: A Problem of Attitude. *Current Archaeology, 39*, 19–45. https://doi.org/10.1086/204697.

Harke, H. (2011). Anglo Saxon Immigration and Ethnogenesis. *Medieval Archaeology, 55*, 1–28. https://doi.org/10.1179/174581711X13103897378311.

Harris, R. (2020). Decolonising the History Curriculum. In M. L. Moncrieffe, R. Race, & R. Harris (Eds.), *Decolonising the Curriculum – Transnational Perspectives. Research Intelligence 142, Spring 2020* (p. 16). London: British Educational Research Association. https://www.bera.ac.uk/publication/spring-2020.

Hawkey, K., & Prior, J. (2011). History, Memory Cultures and Meaning in the Classroom. *Journal of Curriculum Studies, 43*(2), 231–247. https://doi.org/10.1080/00220272.2010.516022.

Lander, V. (2014). Initial Teacher Education: The Practice of Whiteness. In R. Race & V. Lander (Eds.), *Advancing Race and Ethnicity in Education*. Basingstoke: Palgrave Macmillan.

McCrory, C. (2013). How Many People Does It Take to Make an Essex Man? *Teaching History, 152*(September 2013), 8–18.

Ono-George, M. (2019). Beyond Diversity: Anti-Racist Pedagogy in British History Departments. *Women's History Review, 28*(3), 500–507. https://doi.org/10.1080/09612025.2019.1584151.

Runnymede Trust. (2012). *Making Histories: Developing Young Community Historians*. Runnymede Trust On-line Resource. Retrieved August 26, 2014, from http://www.makinghistories.org.uk/

Rüsen, J. (2004). Historical Consciousness: Narrative Structure, Moral Function, and Ontogenetic Development. In P. Seixas (Ed.), *Theorizing Historical Consciousness* (pp. 63–85). Toronto: University of Toronto Press.

Sheldrake, R., & Banham, D. (2007). Seeing a Different Picture: Exploring Migration Through the Lens of History. *Teaching History, 129*(December 2007), 39–47.

Index

A
Acculturation, 70
African-Caribbean, 7, 13, 19, 50, 57, 58, 60–64, 69–72, 78, 83, 85
Afrocentricism, 4
Ajegbo, K., 14
American Civil Rights, 87
Anglo-Saxon invasions, 26
Anti-colonialism, 64
Anti-racist activism, 3

B
Beginning history teachers, 37
Being swamped, 62
Biggest challenge, 7, 26, 42, 89
Black-British children, 19, 62
Black-British experience, 7, 60, 72
Black-British voice, 8
Black cultural icons, 70
Black history, 68
Blackness, 4
Black radicalism, 4
Bob Marley, 67, 70
Bogle, Paul, 64

Boris Johnson, 70
Brexit, 5
Bristol Bus Boycott, 87
British Broadcasting Corporation, 63
Britishness, 14, 82
Brixton 1981, 58, 60–64, 71
Brixton Disorders, 64
Brixton Disturbances, 63
Brixton Road, 63

C
Cameron, David, 28
Claudius, 27
Co-existence, 50, 71
Coldharbour Lane, 63
Colonial zero-point, 3, 4
Conservative government, 14
Conservative/Liberal Democrat coalition, 14
Counter-narrative, 51
Covid-19, 6
Critical, 51
Critical curriculum thinking, 3, 87, 89

Critical multicultural education, 4, 52, 55, 84
Cross-cultural encounters, 7, 28, 50, 51, 71, 77, 78, 80, 85
Cross-cultural struggles, 72
Cross-ethnic encounters, 27, 28, 36, 38
Cuffee (Akofi), 64
Cultural backgrounds, 29
Cultural hegemony, 7, 16, 29, 40
Cultural ignorance, 3
Cultural induction, 38
Cultural reproduction, 30
Curriculum implementation, 86, 87

D
Decentre 'whiteness,' 3
Decolonial thinking, 51
Decolonising, 3, 7, 26, 42, 72, 77, 89
Default perspective, 26
Default position, 4, 7, 26, 42, 78, 89
Defiance of racism, 87
Definition of racism, 27
Deportation, 70
Di Angelo, 26, 27, 29
Diaspora, 70
Diasporic imagination, 70
Discrimination, 62, 69, 70
Diversification, 4
Diversity of societies, 49
Dominant narratives, 52
Duggan, Mark, 67

E
Educational site, 29
Empire, 15, 28, 53
Enoch Powell, 62
Enough is enough!, 66
Epistemic discomfort, 3
Epistemic innovation, 3
Epistemic violence, 7, 19
Epistemological struggle, 3
Equality, 50, 82

Equality Act (2010), 50
Essentialist discourses, 4
Ethnic nationalism, 5
Ethnocentric attitudes, 3
Ethnogenesis, 18, 27, 86
Eurocentric mindset, 7, 26, 40, 42, 78, 89
Eurocentrism, 4, 7, 18, 48, 50, 53, 59, 70, 81, 89
Exemplary, 48

F
Family background, 29
Feeling alien in Britain, 68
First generation, 57
Focus-Group, 78
Freedom of speech, 82
Fundamental British values, 51, 82–84, 88

G
Garvey, Marcus, 64
Genetic, 48, 51, 54, 55, 89
Gentrification, 70
Gestural-superficial, 3, 4
Get up! Stand up!, 69
Gove, Michael, 15
The Grandville Arcade, 63

H
Habitus, 29
Hegemonic normality, 27
Historical consciousness, 7, 47, 48, 51, 52, 54
Historical enquiry, 16, 78, 80, 81, 86
Historicity, 47

I
Imposed epistemes, 51
Initial Teacher Education, 87

Institutional ignorance, 70
Institutional racism, 14
Interactive introspection, 69
Irish, 39

J
Jamaica, 57, 64–66, 68, 70

K
Key Stage 2 history curriculum, 15, 18, 19, 26, 27, 30, 34, 40, 42, 48, 49, 51, 53, 54, 58, 71, 78, 79, 81, 83
Key Stage 3, 18, 50, 53, 55

L
Lawrence, Stephen, 14, 67
Legacy, 18, 52, 59, 68, 70
Legendary rebellions, 64
Lens of migration status, 86
Lived experiences, 29
Loughborough Park, 63

M
Macpherson, W., 14
Macpherson inquiry, 67
Majoritarian ethnic group, 26
The Maroons, 64
Mass-migration and settlement, 13, 16, 18, 19, 26, 27, 33, 34, 39, 41, 42, 49, 50, 53, 54, 60, 69, 78, 83
Master narrative, 15, 16, 29
May, Theresa, 70
Memories, 7, 58, 60, 64, 65, 78
Metropolitan Police Force, 62
Monarchy, 42, 53, 55, 88
Morant Bay, Jamaica, 64
Multicultural co-existence, 6
Multicultural perspectives, 83
Multi-ethnic neighbourhoods, 39
Mutual respect, 5, 51, 88

N
Narcissistic, 2
Nation building, 17
National curriculum chronology, 17
National identity, 17
Nature of history, 26, 42
Neo-conservative, 15
Neo-liberal projects, 5
New Labour government, 14
Non-statutory guidance, 17, 50, 59
Normans, 53, 55, 66, 88
Notting Hill riots, 67

O
Oppression, 4, 64, 69, 70
Optional study, 59
Optional unit, 17, 79
Our Island Story, 15

P
Paradigm, 4
Parks, Rosa, 87
Pedagogical motives, 30
Permanent settlement, 66
Poisonous discourse, 62
Police harassment, 67
Potato famine, 38–39
Power dynamic, 83
Privileged, 26
Privileged 'white' perspective, 26
Process of change, 49
Purpose of Study, 8, 16, 49, 51, 54, 58, 59, 71, 79, 83, 88

Q
Quackoo (Akweku), 64
Quashie (Akwesi), 64
Quintus Lollius Urbicus, 26

R

Race-equality, 4, 7, 14, 16, 63, 71, 87
Race-Relations Acts, 50
Radical, 3, 4, 8, 60
Regime of truth, 29
Reification, 29
Revenge swamping, 62
Revolt, 63
Revolutionary, 3, 4
'Rhodes must fall,' 3
The Roman Empire, 26
The Runnymede Trust, 86
Rüsen, J., 48

S

Scots invasions, 26
Secondary schools, 18, 36, 50
Sense of own identity, 49
7/7 London terrorist attacks, 14
Severus, Septimius, 26
Slave martyrs, 64
Slave revolt, 64
Socialisation, 29, 30, 33–36, 39, 42, 52–54, 70, 87, 88
Sociological imagination, 69
'Statutory' directives, 18
Stephenson, Paul, 87
Stopping and searching, 61, 62, 66
Story of Britain's past, 7, 16, 18, 26, 38, 42, 48, 71, 78, 83, 89
Structural racism, 2
Supplementary Saturday schools, 3
Swamp 1981, 62

T

Temporary settlement, 66
Thatcher, Margaret, 62
Tolerance, 5, 51, 83, 88
Tosh, Peter, 70
Traditional, 48
Trainee-teachers of primary school history, 59, 78, 83
Treaties, 50

U

Unconscious bias training, 4
Undercover racism, 67
Uprisings, 50, 63, 64

V

Viking and Anglo-Saxon struggle, 17, 49, 79
Viking invaders, 26
Vilification and 'othering,' 8
Violence and bloodshed, 69
Visualizing praxis, 80

W

White narcissism, 5
White privilege, 26, 30, 42
White-British majoritarian priorities, 29
White-British propagandas, 26, 42
White-cultural perspectives, 5
White-denial, 87
Whiteness, viii, 2–4, 6–8, 27–30, 42, 72
Whitewashing, 70
Why is my Curriculum White Campaign?, 3
Windrush Generation, 50
Windrush Scandal, 5, 69
Windrush Square, 67

Printed in Great Britain
by Amazon